FAITH
HANGING BY A THREAD

A TRUE STORY ABOUT TRAGEDY,
FORGIVENESS AND RESTORATION

BRYAN I. YAMASHITA

BRYAN I. YAMASHITA

Copyright © 2019 by BRYAN I. YAMASHITA

ISBN: 978-1-946106-53-7

All rights reserved. No part of this publication may be reproduced, distributed, or transmitted in any form or by any means, including photocopying, recording, or other electronic or mechanical methods, without the prior written permission of the publisher, except in the case of brief quotations embodied in critical reviews and certain other noncommercial uses permitted by copyright law. For permission requests, write to the publisher, addressed "Attention: Permissions Coordinator," to BYamashita4@gmail.com.

Scripture quotations are taken from the Holy Bible, New Living Translation, copyright ©1996, 2004, 2015 by Tyndale House Foundation. Used by permission of Tyndale House Publishers, a Division of Tyndale House Ministries, Carol Stream, Illinois 60188. All rights reserved.

Ordering Information:
Logos Bookstore of Hawaii, Inc.
(Halekauwila St., Ste A)
Honolulu., HI. 96813
Ph. 808-596-8890   Fax 808-593-1850
Toll Free Neighbor Isle 1-800-303-1533
Email: logos@logosbookstorehawaii.com

Printed in the United States of America

GLORIFIED PUBLISHING
PO Box 8004
The Woodlands TX 77387
www.GlorifiedPublishing.com

DEDICATION

To the memory of
Asa Shimabukuro Yamashita,
a child and woman of God,
who loved God above all.

BRYAN I. YAMASHITA

CONTENTS

Acknowledgements		ix
Foreword		xi
Introduction		xiii
THE TRAGEDY AND A THREE LEGGED TABLE		**1**
1	February 27, 2009, Friday	3
2	February 28, 2009, Saturday, The Next Day	11
3	March 1, 2009, Sunday, The Third Day	13
4	March 2, 2009, The Impromptu Memorial and Final Viewing	17
5	March 3, 2009, The Candlelight Vigil at Waianae High School	23
6	Do I Need To Forgive God?	27
7	Take This Cup Away	31
8	My Brothers	33
9	A Family In Christ: The Misakis	35
10	Meeting To Plan The Memorial Service With Pastor Eric, and "a little glory to shine through"	37
11	Interview With Dan Nakaso, Reporter from The Honolulu Advertiser	39
12	The Memorial Service	43

13	Church Support	47
14	Gifts	51
15	Along Came A Man Named John	55
16	Bringing Back Some Normalcy For The Girls	59
17	My Going Back To Work	63
18	On Single Parenting	65

FORGIVENESS AND FAITH 73

19	Forgiveness	75
20	What Is Forgiveness?	85
21	Summer of 2009	89
22	The Meaning Of Sacrifice	91
23	Dreams and Premonitions	93

RESTORATION AND HOPE 97

24	Getting Married Again	99
25	A Real Date- Lunch	105
26	Meeting The Girls	109
27	The Proposal	111
28	The Wedding	113
29	Losing Thelma Chun	117

30	Life Changes That Cause Stress	119
31	Happily Ever After- Not	123
32	Spiritual Support	125
33	A Special Mahalo (Thanks)	127
34	The Last Word	129
	Appendix	131

ACKNOWLEDGEMENTS

Before all, and above all, I thank God for helping me write this book. It was not long after our tragedy that I felt I needed to write about what happened; to write about how God showed up in so many ways and revealed his love to the girls and me. I believe it was always His story, and not mine, as it's ultimately more about Him and not about me. Which is how it should be.

When I retired from my teaching career, I thought it would be a good time to start writing this book since I obviously had more time, but as time went on I began to feel that writing this book was not necessary. I just wanted to do my own thing and live a quiet life. That all changed when I had an email conversation with a dear friend who expressed his great concern for a loved one who survived a very traumatic time in her life, which caused painful memories that just would not subside. I knew when I finished this conversation that my story needed to be written, especially to help those with wrongs that they suffered in their past.

In Easter of 2017 my senior pastor Norman Nakanishi of Grace Bible Church Pearlside had me share my testimony again with our church services. As we waited in the green room before the first service, he said I needed to write this story. Not an hour later an associate pastor, who was not with us, also said the same thing. That was confirmation enough that I needed to write this book. Again I thank God for getting me to write this book, as I wrote this book out of obedience to Him.

Aside from my Father in Heaven I want to especially thank the following people who were of great help in publishing this book:

- My brother Boyden Yamashita, his son Kelii Yamashita, and dear friends Nancy Young, June Honda Misaki, and Carl Ashizawa for their editing and or reviewing of the book.

-Tim and Cora De Mello for writing the foreword and their unwavering support from the beginning, and their daughter Alyssa for allowing me to include her poem in the book that was shared at Asa's memorial service.

-My dear wife Cathy and my daughters Katie and Tori, and the Calvin and Thelma Chun family for allowing me to share their personal lives with others.

-Shaun Castro for the incredible hand-drawn cover illustration.

-Brad Goda for our family portrait on the back cover at Kapapapuhi Point Park.

-My small (prayer) group: Aaron Chan, Virgil Salvador for their faithful prayers through the last two years of writing this book.

I especially thank Edie Bayer of Kingdom Promoters (www.KingdomPromoters.org) and her expertise for her final editing, text formatting, cover design, advising, and assistance in publishing this book.

I also respectfully acknowledge Asa's family's request that they not be mentioned in this book.

FOREWORD

My friend Bryan.

I am blessed to have a friend like Bryan. He lost his wife many years ago and I was there to witness his walk of faith with God. I still remember the night that I found out about the tragedy. My brother heard it on the news early that evening. I called Bryan and he remarked, "I'm so grateful that I don't have any anger."

What? That's not the response that I was expecting! His response to what happened and all the situations I saw him in was the same - an unlikely response to what humans would typically do, but what a Christian walking out his faith should look like.

That uncommon walk helped prepare me for the stroke that I was to have and the loss of both of our moms in the same year. During those events, my reliance on God and walking out my faith helped tremendously, just as Bryan had done. My family and I thank the Lord for carrying us through the difficult times. It sure helped to see how our friend did it, walking out his faith, through the loss of Asa. It is amazing to see how far he and his kids, Katie and Tori, have come. Praise Jesus.

So, God in His majesty, grace and extravagant love helped

prepare me for what was to come in my life. I've seen Bryan coach basketball, and even golf with one hand, marveling at how much he had overcome to get where he is now. These days he has become our "yard man" - coming to our home on a monthly basis with all his stuff. He comes prepared! Plus, now, his eldest daughter Katie is planning to go away to college. This is a storybook ending of how far this family has come.

I see God in all of this and look forward to helping in any way that I can. So birth forward the scholarship giving. That's how God works! He grows out the seeds that are about Him. Whatever His kids do, God is going to bless them as long as their hearts are about Him. And that is what God does. He works out all things for our good, according to His plan. ROMANS 8:28.

We thank You, Lord, in advance for all that You are going to do in our lives. Thank you Bryan for being a great example of how one should walk out his faith. Praise Jesus. Amen.

Tim De Mello

INTRODUCTION

At the time of our tragedy, Asa was in her tenth year as a teacher at Waianae High School in Waianae, Hawaii. After teaching English in the classroom for a few years she became the school's Literacy Coach and Coordinator. She was charged with assisting all teachers and working directly with students to foster interest in and to improve reading skills. She deeply believed that improved literacy skills were fundamental to achieving overall academic success in every area of study.

We were married for sixteen years and made our home in Ewa Beach, Hawaii. I was teaching Social Studies at Nanakuli Intermediate and High School. Katie was only seven. She was in the second grade at Holomua Elementary School. Tori was four years old and was at Seagulls Schools Kapolei. On Saturdays the girls played soccer in the AYSO West Oahu Division. On Sundays we worshipped at Pearl City Community Church.

On that fateful day, when Asa was attacked, I believe she did her best to save her life. I imagine in that moment she was thinking about how much her daughters needed her, as she did her best to parry the blows, even while seeking refuge in a nearby store. Asa not only cared deeply for our daughters, myself, and her family, she cared deeply for her whole school. She cared deeply for literacy for all people; she cared deeply for her friends and her church. Most of all, she loved God above everything else. And through it all, God was with her every step of the way. He was always with her, as He promises, because He is faithful.

My name is Bryan I. Yamashita. It is through my experience that I tell this story, which I believe, ultimately, is God's story.

THE TRAGEDY AND A THREE LEGGED TABLE

BRYAN I. YAMASHITA

CHAPTER ONE

February 27, 2009, Friday

February 27th, 2009 was a Friday. It was a good day as Fridays should go. It was special because Katie had a fun run fundraiser at her school, where kids earn money by running around the school campus. Asa took the day off to chaperone and cheer for Katie and the other children.

After the school event, Asa planned to go to the Ewa Town Shopping Center for a dental appointment and get a haircut; however, she called me in the middle of my class to tell me that her car wouldn't start. I said, "Just walk to the shopping center and wait for me to pick you up later." Then she said something intriguing: "This is turning out to be a really bad day." That was the last time we spoke.

Later, after I left my school and got to the shopping center, there seemed to be some confusion. I could see police tape fronting the area where I was supposed to pick her up. After I parked the car a little ways away, my heart started to race as I drew closer to the Ewa Seed store. I started to sense that something was terribly wrong.

Suddenly I received a phone call. Thinking it was Asa I quickly answered the phone. Instead, I heard a woman's voice asking for me, telling me that my wife was in cardiac arrest at St. Francis West Hospital. Hanging up, I thought, "How can this be since she is in good health?" I turned around and went back to my car.

I was trying to get to the hospital as soon as possible, but there I was, crawling on the road since it was a Friday afternoon, in bad traffic. My heart started to race and my breathing quickened as I began to feel a sense of panic. Suddenly, I had a vision of the scene from the movie *Castaway* where Tom Hanks' character, in a moment of desperation, tells himself to, *"just breathe."* So I did. I took deep breaths, gradually calming myself down.

After a time I finally got to the hospital. Running into the emergency room, I was directed into a side waiting room where some workers were finishing their lunch. As they left a police officer came in to talk to me. The young officer apologized for my loss, saying Asa was attacked and killed by a man. He added that they had apprehended this man. I remember thinking only that Asa really was dead and that it really happened.

Strangely, about six months prior, I began having recurring thoughts of what life would be like without Asa. These thoughts would occur when my mind would wander especially when I was washing the dishes. I would ponder the thought of life without her for a moment and then shake it from my mind since life without her would be impossible.

On Sunday of that week something strange started to happen. I started to feel a disconnection between Asa and myself. It made me sad. After a while I told her that for some strange reason, I felt we were growing apart. Actually this feeling had started earlier, but on that Sunday night it felt very intense...so much so that I had to talk to her about it.

Later, after she had put the girls to bed, we had a moment in the kitchen and I told her what I was feeling, but I could not explain why. Nothing gave cause to this feeling of separation, but I needed to tell her I still loved her. She shrugged her shoulders and said she loved me too. We hugged each other briefly and then she went up to go to bed. But for some reason I could not sleep in the bed with her. I just felt I had to sleep on the couch downstairs, something I had never done before. I did that for the rest of the week, too. I believe it was God moving us apart in preparation for what was to come.

Now, here I was - in the emergency room, waiting, after the police officer told me she had died. I said to myself, "Wow! It really happened! Now we are truly separated." While I was there, the hospital staff said I had to identify her body; but, because her body was now evidence for a crime, I had to identify her by viewing a digital camera image. In other words, they would not allow me to see her in person. They brought a camera to me and showed me a picture of her - but just her head with a breathing mask on. I confirmed that it was her.

As I left the hospital, the staff stopped to stare at me, like they were worried I would make a scene. As I left the doors of the emergency room to get to the parking lot I was suddenly blinded by the bright afternoon light. I staggered a little, and then I felt like the whole world disappeared for a moment. It was as if I was caught in a white fog.

I said a short prayer..."God please help me." Then for a moment there was nothing. It was just me and God. I felt as if my life was hanging by a thread. At any moment I felt I could just lose it, but I didn't because this thread - or whatever it was - was holding me. It did not fail. The fog disappeared and I got in the car.

From there I went to pick up my daughter Katie from her after school program. I asked myself, *What am I going to say to her? How am I going to tell the girls about what happened?* When I got to Katie's school I tried my best to tell the program director that the girls may be out for a while. Katie looked up at me and asked me what was wrong. I looked down and said, "Something really bad happened today." She asked, "Why, did mom die?"

What? How could she know? I looked down at her and thought to myself, "*Well, I never want to start lying to you, kid,*" so I said, "Yes, she died today." More questions ensued but all I could say was I don't know and that someone had attacked her.

Katie started crying hard as I went to get Tori from her preschool. As we got closer to Tori's school I came up with the idea of asking Katie to take Tori aside to give her the bad news herself. I think I just thought it would give her something to do. Katie started to calm down. After I signed Tori out I told the school staff, too, that she may be out for a few days.

Coming home in the car both girls were screaming in stereo. It was so hurtful to hear their wailings. When we got home Katie asked permission to go to her room to continue crying to which I said yes. Tori went into the living room. I went to my room to rest; I just felt exhausted.

One of the first phone calls I got was from my union president, Roger Takabayashi, who was actually my shop teacher when I was in middle school. I don't know how he got the news, but he caringly expressed his condolences and asked if there was anything he could do. I thought of nothing but thanked him for the call. A few months later when our union had its state convention in Waikiki he gave me and the girls his penthouse suite for a day, which was the biggest upgrade I had ever had in my life.

Some family started showing up and then my brothers and their wives. In my heart I began to yearn for Christian fellowship. Finally, my brother Boyden, a minister, and his wife, Angel, a strong believer who had brought my brother to Christ many years before, showed up in my driveway. I remember walking straight to her door to greet her then hugging her and whispering, "God is good."

As the evening progressed, I answered phone call after phone call. There were many times I received calls while I was on the phone but I didn't put anyone on hold. I talked to as many people as I could. The girls were well cared for, as there seemed to be almost a festive atmosphere in the house. I could not eat. I was in shock.

Later, when it was bath time, I took the girls up one by one not knowing how to do it, as Asa had always done the bathing. There we stood in the bathroom, Katie naked and looking up at me; me looking down at her, saying, "Okay, how do we do this?" However, with the girls' help we got it all done.

From then on, among all other things, I became solely in charge of their care. Some days later the girls began to complain that Asa was much more gentle during bath time, to which I replied, "I wash you two like I wash my car: I just get it done." That night Tori did something rather disturbing during bath time. She played with the bath crayons and smeared the red one over the walls of the tub. It actually looked like blood after a while. I suddenly told her to stop playing with it. I wonder what she was thinking. After I got the girls to bed I felt really tired so I told my family to please go home.

I tried to sleep but could not; I was so wired from what happened. After a while of tossing in bed I went downstairs to watch TV. The very first thing I saw on the television was the scene from the movie *Castaway* which I had thought of earlier in the day, trying to get from the shopping center to the hospital, while taking deep breaths to calm myself down. It was the exact same scene I had been thinking about in the car, when the Tom Hanks character tells a friend after he was rescued how he survived while considering suicide on the island by just breathing, breath to breath, just staying alive from moment to moment. At that moment I thought, "Wow! How did this happen?"

Thankfully, after watching the movie for a while I felt sleepy, and I went back to bed. Funny, Tom Hanks movies have a special place in my heart.

February 27th 2009 ends for me.

==================================

What happened to Asa that day:

In the early afternoon, at about 1:30 p.m., Asa was eating a lunch of saimin noodles. She was sitting on a bench at the Ewa Town Center when she was brutally attacked by a stranger named Tittleman Fauatea, a twenty-five year old male who lived near the shopping center. He suddenly attacked her with a newly bought kitchen knife, stabbing her six times. Asa struggled to get away from him by seeking help from a nearby nail salon and collapsed into its entrance. He then walked across the street where he was soon arrested. She was later taken by ambulance to the St. Francis West Hospital where she shortly died.

It was later reported that Fauatea had a history of mental illness since his adolescence and was a patient of the Hawaii State Hospital. It was also reported later that this attack was possibly the result of Fauatea's unaccepted romantic advances towards a worker at a nearby hair cutting shop whom he had mistaken for Asa. Therefore, this attack was also possibly the result of mistaken identity.

CHAPTER TWO

February 28, 2009 Saturday, the next day

I woke up early in the morning at about five a.m. like I normally do, and went downstairs to drink coffee and pray.

When I put the coffee on I turned to walk away and suddenly I felt the whole world come crashing down on my shoulders. It was the extreme weight of the thought of taking care of the girls by myself. I remember thinking when I was at the hospital that it would have been better for the girls to have not been adopted by us since they would have been spared such terrible grief.

In that moment I fell to my knees on the kitchen floor and began to cry out loud, saying, "I cannot take care of them by myself." Asa was everything to the girls. I was just the family driver and the diaper bag carrier. While on my knees, tears gushed out of my eyes as I kept saying out loud, "I cannot take care of them by myself!"

But then a clear, strong audible voice said from behind me, "You CAN." I was so distraught that I realized that I was rocking back and forth on my knees. Every time I said I could not take care of them the voice behind me responded simply, "You CAN." Finally, I said that I couldn't do it just to hear the voice again say it once more, "You CAN." It was then that I felt this warm sensation on my back like a big hand was on me, filling me, strengthening me. After a while I got up, wiped the tears from my face and went to pray.

I know who that voice was. It had to be from God. He spoke to me clearly, challenging my "no confidence in myself" for taking care of the girls. In retrospect, God was saying that I can take care of the girls, not by myself, but with His help, every step of the way. What he was calling me to do was simply to trust in Him. And in prayer and every waking moment I continued to trust in him. As I continued to believe and trust in God, he continued to bless, provide, and guide me through every moment during this crisis.

I woke up the girls and after feeding them breakfast, people started to come. Family and friends came by to give their condolences and offer support. Again the constant flow of phone calls, one after the other kept coming in. Then there were news reports from the TV about what happened. It seemed to be known everywhere.

CHAPTER THREE

March 1, 2009 Sunday, The Third Day

Last night the girls wanted to sleep in my room. I could tell they were afraid and they needed to be near me.

I woke up in bed at about five a.m. and suddenly I felt so terribly sad I started to cry. I lay there talking to Asa as if she were there, saying how sorry I was that she had to die such a horrible death. I sobbed that I could not save her or even take her place as I would have.

As I lay in bed weeping, I remembered the girls were on the other side of the bed sleeping on the carpet. I got up quietly and walked over to check on them. I stood there, looking down at my daughters. I noticed that Katie was watching me, probably awakened by my crying. She got up as I bent down and came over to give me a big hug. She said, "Daddy, it's going to be rough for a few days." I cried even more as my daughter consoled me. After a while I told her to return to sleep while I went downstairs to pray.

On this day, fewer people came to the house. In the afternoon my pastors Eric Ebisu and Keith Young came to visit and pray with and for me. I really needed to meet with a retired teacher and friend Jimmy Higa who agreed to be my substitute for a few weeks. He was great as he took over my classes which allowed me to take care of the girls and plan for Asa's memorial service. I met Jimmy at a fast food restaurant near his home and we briefly went over what I needed him to do. He assured me that he would take care of everything. He did just as he said he would, because later when I came back to school, it was really like I was just there.

I decided to keep the girls at home for a week and then in the following week to just attend soccer practices and games. I felt it was important to normalize our lives as soon as possible. Staying home, away from life's activities, makes it harder to get back into it the longer you're away. I guess it's like what they say about falling off a horse.

Soon we heard that Asa's friends from Waianae High School were planning a candlelight vigil in her memory. Asa's dearest friend from work, Kat Muranaka, contacted me to invite us to the vigil which was happening on a Tuesday evening. I thought okay, I'll just show up. Later she asked if I would say a few words to the people. I thought okay, I'll say just a few words.

The story of Asa's death was all over the TV news. I watched with some amusement, wondering why was there so much public interest? It seemed to me to be more of a very personal tragedy. People seemed surprised about my comments and thoughts of forgiveness for my wife's killer. Not that I shouldn't be angry, it was just that this tragedy was so surreal and that it didn't make any sense. It seemed to me hard to get angry about something that just did not make sense.

My daily and main concerns were simply to care for my girls, provide for my students, and plan and organize the needed tasks to bury my beloved wife. I also viewed the media as a way to communicate to family and friends that we were okay. I knew so many people were trying to contact me. I also began to understand that the Christian Community around the island was praying for us, and I definitely could feel their prayers. We are so grateful for their many prayers.

CHAPTER FOUR

March 2, 2009, Monday

The Impromptu Memorial and Final Viewing

Today, I decided to take the girls to the impromptu flower memorial that was created at the spot of Asa's attack, the bench outside of the Ewa Seed Store. It seemed people were so moved by what happened that they brought and laid flowers at the site. I planned to have the girls choose some flowers from a nearby grocery store and lay them down as well.

Strangely, as we got out of the car in the parking lot, I began to feel very defensive, constantly looking around at our surroundings. It was as if I was fearing another attack. Thankfully, this feeling subsided after a while. In the parking lot, I bumped into a mother of Katie's classmates who also brought flowers to the memorial. There were lots of flowers of all kinds. I learned later that the owner of the Ewa Seed Company, whom my daughters and I simply call Uncle Dean (Hashimoto), regularly watered and tended to the flowers as best he could. He was one of the last people to see her alive.

The girls and I laid the flowers there and I said a short prayer. The area was pretty clean. All of the blood that was shed was washed away. I now believe God saved me from seeing all that blood, since I received that phone call from the hospital just before I got close to the scene on that fateful day. Seeing all that blood would have been greatly disturbing.

The Ewa Seed Company was mostly a shaved-ice store which also sold assorted snacks and goodies. It remains, as always, a special place for us even after the tragedy. We frequent the store, eating our favorite flavors, sitting at the same spot where Asa was attacked. I do this because I don't want the girls to lose a place that brings joy them. I do this because we claim this place in the name of Jesus Christ, our Sovereign LORD, and that we do not let the devil lay claim to it.

To this day, I know people who will not even go there in sympathy of what happened that day. In fact, rumors were spreading that I would sell our house to move somewhere else, and therefore move the girls to another school. At a school function, the girl's school principal approached me about this and I assured him we were not leaving the district. Holomua Elementary School was our school.

I didn't get upset at these rumors since I think it would make sense for people who experience something like this to leave and live somewhere far away. Maybe there is a need or desire to start life anew somewhere else.

Speaking of moving, one night about two weeks later as I was putting the girls down to sleep, my second daughter Tori suddenly sat up in her bed, very upset. She asked me, "What is going to happen to us?" Confused, I asked her what she meant. She responded, "Where are we, (she and Katie) going to live?"

Suddenly, I realized what she was asking. She was thinking that our life together was over and our family would be broken up; that we would become separated. Perhaps she thought she and Katie would be sent back to China, where both of my girls were adopted. As Katie intently listened too, I calmly told the girls, in as clear a voice as possible, that nothing in our lives changes, except that mom is not here. I ardently said, "We live in the same house, you go to the same school, we play soccer on the same teams, and we go to the same church on Sundays. Nothing changes." She stared at me for a moment before saying "Okay". Then she laid down and soon went to sleep.

As I lay beneath their loft beds that night while waiting for them to fall asleep, I believe the Lord gave me a vision of a four-legged table suddenly losing one leg, with the three remaining legs adjusting to become a three-legged table. The girls and I would become like that three-legged table. What we would need to do was adjust and accept what happened, and we would be okay.

Later that morning, following the impromptu memorial, we had scheduled the final viewing of Asa's body with the mortuary. This viewing was to be done prior to her body being cremated. It would only be for the immediate family: the girls and I, other family, and my brothers and their wives.

For me, the body viewing is really a formality of the mortuary process. My belief is that after death the body becomes only an earthly shell that was formerly inhabited by the spirit and soul of the person, which is really who the person is. So I guess seeing her body for the last time was not a big deal for me. I knew and know where Asa is - the heavenly realm we who believe are destined to.

I was curious to see how the girls would react to seeing her lifeless body. Thankfully, the people at the mortuary had made good use of the dresses I delivered for the viewing process and they had done her makeup very well. I was afraid of how she would look since the killer stabbed and cut her multiple times. But here she looked beautiful and well, lying in the viewing coffin with her hands folded, covered by a bouquet of flowers. It was good to see her looking so beautiful, considering the way she was killed.

When Katie came up to view the body, she ran her hands all over Asa, making sure she had died. Tori, on the other hand, came up and simply stared at her, looking up and down her entire body, not touching her at all. Both girls remained calm and did not cry at this last look. Maybe it was because I shared my thoughts on death with them earlier ... that their mom was not really there and that we were just seeing her body for the last time.

As other family members came up to see Asa's body I started humming to the background music that was playing, which I recognized and liked. Tori, upon hearing me, at some point turned to me and said, "Stop." Oh well! Nothing like getting disciplined by your four-year old daughter.

I do want to share a timely event involving the mortuary that really made an impression on me. Later on, that same week, I had to go back to meet with the funeral representative who had been such an incredible help for the memorial service. I was a little early for the morning meeting so I took a short walk around the grounds.

Near one of the buildings was a large Banyan tree that, upon examination, I noticed had a large branch cut. It appeared that the tree was in the slow process of growing its bark back over the cut. I could see that the bark was on its way to healing the entire cut area, but it would take months - if not years - to completely heal from the great pruning that had taken place.

As I studied the tree I realized that we, too, had experienced a great wound, one that would take a long time to heal. Yet, even completely healed, there would be a scar that would still forever remain. Our tragedy would never be forgotten by us.

It is said that when we see Jesus again, evidence of the wounds in his hands from his crucifixion will remain as well. But with God's grace we, too, will be healed like this tree one day. Yes, I decided...we are like this tree. I praise God for the incredible ways He shows up and speaks to us of His love and, in this case, His healing power. Now, I always look for the work of His hands and His guarding arms. Some people call these "God moments."

CHAPTER FIVE

March 3, 2009 Tuesday,

The Candlelight Vigil at Waianae High School

I really didn't know what to expect at this event. I was hoping it would be a small informal gathering and that I would just say a few words. Well, I was learning, things don't always go like you expect.

That evening as we were heading out to Waianae I started to get anxious about what I would say, given the opportunity, as I had nothing prepared. Then, a song on the Christian radio station K-Love, called *Word of God Speak* by Mercy Me, came on and it told me not to fear about what I would need to say; but, rather, to trust God and that He would provide the words. I calmed down and noted some talking points on a piece of paper.

There were a lot of people already there when we arrived. A parking space had been reserved for us and we could see candles lit at the flagpole. As it was starting to get dark we walked into the cafeteria where we were escorted to chairs in the front. The television media were all there. The room began to fill up, with many more people standing outside, looking in through the louvers.

Asa's friends, led by Kat Muranaka, came up to start the program. They produced a slideshow of Asa at school, and it was very heartwarming. There were a multitude of images of

Asa interacting with students, teachers, and staff. You could just see in your mind her book cart, and hear the pitter-patter of her quick step throughout the hallways.

As mentioned before, Asa was the school's literacy coach, which was a non-classroom, teaching position. She serviced all teachers and classrooms in an effort to promote reading and literacy skills among the students. It was the general consensus among those in educational circles at that time that improved reading skills led to improved overall academic and future success. This concept was the driving force behind all of Asa's efforts.

As the program went underway I noticed that, while Katie was immersed in some book, Tori seemed to be taking it all in. After the slideshow the planners had a group of former graduates share what Asa meant to them. They were a proud group of honor students and they spoke so fondly of Asa. Their perspective was heartwarming! They spoke from the position of those who have graduated appreciating the good work of their teachers a few years later. They shared from their hearts about what Asa did for them, and what she meant to them. It was truly inspiring. A staff worker at the school also spoke about how Asa encouraged her to read because everyone's reading skills, those of students and staff, mattered to Asa.

When these people were done I was asked to speak. I first thanked everyone who came and especially those who had shared earlier. I then told a story about how Asa and I had been shopping at a large bulk store, and she bought up all the *Twilight* books on the shelf. These books were hugely popular at that time. She would then take the books to school, and just hand them out to students and staff to read on their own, requesting that they pass them on to someone else interested in the books.

I shared another memory about Asa taking a particular interest in a certain boy who had openly declared his hatred of reading. Asa later discovered that he loved skateboarding, so she shopped at a bookstore for a book on the topic. She found a book that was expensive and asked me if she should buy it. I told her that anything that could get that boy interested in reading would be worth it.

The next week while visiting that student's class she strategically placed the book on her reading cart where he could see it and then handed the book to the boy. She watched the boy intently as he picked up the book and ran up the gym bleachers to snuggle up with it. The book had lots of pictures but he was reading it as well.

Finally, I shared about Asa's death; how terrible it was, and how we were all hurting from the loss. However, I told the people not to get angry at what happened, because acting out in anger really does no good... it only leads to more harm. I told them what they could do, instead, was to find something that needs to be changed either at school, at home, in the community or simply in themselves; and to thoughtfully consider making that change. I said this would be the best way to honor Asa. Then I thanked everyone for coming, saying that I would gladly meet and receive anyone who wanted to see me after the vigil.

And, boy, they did! After the vigil ended I was swarmed by what felt like hundreds of people. I have never felt so many hugs in my life. People crying and speaking words of condolences, some hugging me in their Polynesian way. It was encouraging to receive the outpouring of school and community support.

When the last person said goodbye I packed up the girls and left to go home. I was amazed by what happened that evening. It turned out later that since there was this vigil at Waianae High School, most of the community did not need to come to her memorial service which was held far in town, so this was good.

As I was driving home I realized that what God spoke to me through that song was true! I didn't need to worry about what to say, for I think I was calm and deliberate in speech; that God had provided the words, and like all His promises in the Bible, the Lord keeps His word, for He is faithful.

CHAPTER SIX

Do I Need To Forgive God?

One morning, during the first week after Asa's death, I was on the phone with my brother Boyden. He had called on me to check on me and see how I was doing. After some small talk, I asked him a question that was heavy on my heart. I asked, "Do I need to forgive God for what happened to Asa?" After a brief silence he resolutely replied, "Why? God did not cause Asa's death." But what I meant was this: could God have saved her from being attacked? Boyden replied, "Yes, he could have saved her, but He did not cause her to die."

That was a hard answer with which to come to grips. This is about an age-old question: *Why do bad things happen to good people?* Asa was no angel, but she was as good a person as I have ever met, and she was deeply serious about her faith in God. Yet, she was taken away so suddenly and in the most violent manner one could imagine. Her life was torn away from a family that needed her dearly. Again, this was a tough question I had to grapple with and I know I am not alone. Many people wonder about this as well. It is one of those questions that truly will test your faith.

I am sure this is a question that makes many believers turn away from God. In my case I decided not to turn away, I decided to get closer to God. And true to His word, as I got closer to Him, God got closer to me (James 4:8). As God got closer to me, I was able to experience a kind of joy that I never thought possible.

This is a kind of special joy I believe the Bible speaks about. It's not a happy joy, but rather it is the presence of God that is so close, He is actually on you. This is how I have come to experience and understand what this kind of "joy" means. "J-O-Y" in this sense stands for "**J**esus **O**n **Y**ou." The Lord Jesus is so close to you, he is actually hugging you from behind, sustaining you, firmly but lovingly holding us with his hands when we can no longer stand on our own.

I think this kind of joy was experienced by the apostle Paul when he was in chains in a jail but all the while singing hymns of praise unto the Lord (Acts 16:25). This is what I have experienced since I made a decision to trust in God, no matter what. I felt like Peter when he said to Jesus, "Where else can I go? You have the words that give eternal life." (John 6:68) God alone was there with me in that hospital parking lot and He has never left me (Deuteronomy 31:6). Ever since I made that decision to trust God in all things I have never regretted it.

More than ever, after the tragedy, I've experienced blessings of every magnitude, some small, some big, but all showing me the wonders of His love. Now, I live in quiet anticipation of His goodness and grace being revealed because I now see His hand in so many things! Yet, all He calls me to do is simply *believe*.

I may never understand why Asa died that day, and the truth is, I don't have to. If God wants to reveal the answer to me, that is His will. I still sometimes wonder why it happened but the question does not distract me from my trust in the Lord. Sometimes I hear people say they will understand the reason why things happened in their life when they get to heaven. I think that even when I get there I don't need to know. I just want to be there, in the un-ending presence of Jesus. It will be so awesome! I will have no desire to ask questions. I will just experience His bliss.

So do I need to forgive God? No. The Lord is good, perfect, and loving. Yes, He is all powerful, all knowing, and ever present. He causes no evil act. What I need to do is simply to continue to trust in Him, no matter what.

The following scriptures have supported me to walk through this question:

Isaiah 55: 8-9 **"My thoughts are nothing like your thoughts says the Lord. And my ways are far beyond anything you could imagine. Where just as the heavens are higher than the Earth, so my ways are higher than your ways and my thoughts are higher than your thoughts."**

Isaiah 57:1-2 **"Good people pass away; The godly often die before their time. But no one seems to care or wonder why. No one seems to understand that God is protecting them from the evil to come. For those who follow Godly paths will rest in peace when they die."**

Romans 8:28 **"And we know that God causes all things to work for their good; to those who love God, to those who are called according to his purpose for them."**

CHAPTER SEVEN

Take This Cup Away

On another morning, while I was on the phone with Boyden, I was feeling the weight of everything I had to do. What with the memorial service, the obituary, and everything else, it was just so much! I had to do it, because nobody else could. I had to make so many decisions, completely and utterly alone.

At some point in our conversation I just said that everything was too much! It was a burden that was becoming impossible to carry. I cried out, saying, "I don't want this cup! Take this cup away! I just don't want it." It was one of those moments that the thread of faith I was holding onto felt like it was just getting thinner and thinner, cutting into my hand.

After a while I was able to calm down and finish the phone call. Later, I thought about what I said. I thought about Jesus in the Garden of Gethsemane and how He cried out to God to take His cup of suffering away from Him. I felt very close to Jesus in that moment.

As you can probably understand, I did a lot of crying during that time, since the pain in the aftermath of our loss was so severe. I never had trouble expressing my emotions although I am not an emotional person. I remember crying in the hospital when my father was dying of cancer. My mother tried to console me by asking why I was crying. In almost disbelief that she would ask this question, I remember saying to her, "It's okay Mom. It's just my emotions."

So when Asa died, I cried a lot, even at times when I shared my testimony at church. Just thinking of that time still touches a tender nerve, even after many years. When I think that I have gotten over the emotions of our tragedy, my chest gets tight and the tears start to flow.

Sometimes they don't just flow - the tears actually spray from my eyes! I cry so hard that my glasses get fogged with spray. It's like being at the beach with pounding surf that after a while covers your glasses with wet spots which make them almost unseeable.

Our tragedy was so bad I remember thinking that I would never wish this - what we went through - on anyone.

Not even Asa's killer.

CHAPTER EIGHT

My Brothers

I think it's a good time to share about my family. I have three brothers. I was the third of four. They are Byrnes, Boyden, and Barry. All of our first names begin with the letter "B" and also include both of our initials "B" and "Y." I'm not sure why my parents named us this way but I guess they liked the letter "B." My brothers are great guys, all are married and have grown children of their own.

On the day of the tragedy they all came over to the house. I don't know how they found out about what happened. I guess it was on the news. None called first but they probably tried, as I was constantly on the phone. I remember each one coming. I talked briefly with each of them before welcoming them into the house. I felt I had to privately just tell them that Asa was attacked and killed and that I didn't know how it happened.

But as I mentioned before, it was not until my brother Boyden and his wife Angel arrived that I received a feeling of relief and comfort. When I greeted Angel I was able to softly declare as I hugged her that, "God is good." I'm so glad that I said this, even though I don't know how I could say it given what happened. But I am truly grateful that I could proclaim the goodness of God on that day, even though what happened was just so bad and bizarre. I could take a moment to praise the grace of God.

After several weeks my brother Byrnes sat down with me to talk to me about my financial situation. He said that he and my other brothers would try to help me each month. I had figured out by that time that I would be able to manage and that I would try to take care of our own finances. And the Lord God blessed us with the ability to do that!

I was so grateful to have family to help me in any way that we needed. Barry was a great help as he would occasionally come over bringing bags of groceries and offering to do odd jobs around the house. Byrnes would come over once a month for over a year to cut my grass and help me regrow it in areas where I had brown patches of dirt. Today my yard is great because of his work.

But the one that made the greatest impact on a daily basis was my brother Boyden. This brother of mine, on top of his full-time job as an administrator and dentist for the V.A. Hospital and minister at his church, would call me every morning at about 6:30 a.m. to check on how I was doing each day, even on weekends. We would both share how we were doing and offer a prayer over both of our days.

I am so grateful that he took the time to do this every day for three straight years, but I have to admit, sometimes he called at the most difficult times! Sometimes he called when I was trying to either cook breakfast and feed the girls, or simply trying to get all of us ready for school and work. At the end of three years he finally decided that I would be okay and that he didn't have to call me every day. I thought I would be okay, too! What a great brother.

CHAPTER NINE

A Family in Christ - The Misakis

At the memorial service, a family from Pearl City Community Church offered to sit with the girls outside of the service in case they had trouble sitting through it. This was really helpful for Katie because she seemed uncomfortable about the whole service. Plus, I had a feeling it would take so long to greet people afterward. When I offered this opportunity to the girls they grabbed it!

We call this family the Misakis. This family consists of mother June, daughter Kristen and son Kory; grandpa Mitsuo and grandma Millie Honda; June's boyfriend Sheldon Yano, and many dear family friends that have loved the girls as their own family.

June was also the assistant director of Sunday School and a teacher at our church. For about three years after the tragedy this family would take care of the girls every Sunday from the time church service ended until evening after dinner. This was an incredible blessing, because it allowed me time to take care of all my chores like cleaning the house, yard work and doing the laundry each week. Their help also allowed me much-needed time alone to just be by myself. This was the generous help they provided on a weekly basis.

This family filled the girls' Sunday afternoons with a multitude of excursions, and would include the girls in dinner planning and preparation at their home. All I had to do was pick up the girls, bring them home and put them into bed. This great act of love and sacrifice gave me and the girls so much help I cannot emphasize it enough!

What was a great concern to me then was - What would happen during Christmas? How could I make this special holiday a happy event for the girls? But then came the Misaki's. It would begin with Aunty June having the girls write Santa Claus letters from which a shopping list was derived. The family would shop and wrap all the gifts and invite us to their annual Christmas party on the eve. At the end of the night they would secretly transfer all the gifts into my car trunk to be placed under our tree after I put them to bed. All I had to do was cut them a check for all the gifts for the girls. Plus, the family gave gifts from themselves, of course.

Christmas morning would be filled with screams of joy and laughter. I cannot thank or give more credit to this family! They made Christmas good at our house and probably did far more than what Asa and I could have done by ourselves. Today, Christmas is the girls' favorite holiday. I know it was because of this incredible family. I also know that Christmas could have been the girls' worst holiday considering our tragedy.

Without a a doubt, I know in my heart that God touched this family to help me and the girls. May our Sovereign Lord always bless them in innumerable ways. Aloha Misakis.

CHAPTER TEN

Meeting To Plan The Memorial Service With Pastor Eric and "a little glory to shine through"

In preparation for Asa's memorial service I asked my Pastor Eric Ebisu if he would preside over the service. He said he would be glad to help. My brother Boyden, being a minister himself at his church, would also help in the service.

We all met together one evening at the Pearl City Community Church office. Before we started the planning session, Pastor Eric opened in prayer, humbly asking God for "a little of His glory" to shine through during this time.

A few days later, after I went to bed, I was probably sleeping for an hour when I had a dream of a bright light, the brightest LIGHT I have ever seen in my life, shining from high above. It was like it was coming down from a helicopter but there was no helicopter or sound. It was like a bright searchlight that beamed from above, cutting through the complete darkness of the night.

In the next moment of this dream I was outside on my driveway, standing just outside of the presence of this incredible light. Suddenly, Katie appeared from the shadows and stretched out her hand to touch the light. Out of great fear I screamed, "Katie, No! Stay out of the light!". At that moment I jumped up out of my bed, hyperventilating about the whole experience. Later the next morning I told Boyden about what happened and he chuckled, "Brother, that was a little of that glory Pastor Eric prayed for - remember?"

I guess it was and I wondered why it happened. To this day I believe it was God showing me the power of His glory through this light, a light that is so powerful, it's truly scary. And that's why I yelled at Katie to stay out of it. God's glory is a fearful thing that demands extreme respect and amazement. The LORD showed me a glimpse of His glory, His sovereignty and power. These were forever established in my heart.

CHAPTER ELEVEN

Interview With Dan Nakaso, Reporter From The Honolulu Advertiser

That week I also met with a reporter from the Honolulu Advertiser, a newspaper which was still in print at that time. His name was Dan Nakaso and he said he wanted to do a story about me. I first thought, "Why me? This thing was not about me, it was about Asa." But he said, "No. People want to know about *YOU*."

I said okay and we met. I answered his questions and shared some pictures. The photographer he brought along just happened to be a guy from way back in high school that I wrestled against. The photographer he brought along was very pleasant as he quietly admired my family pictures before he carefully took his photographs. He quietly asked a few questions himself.

When Dan was satisfied with our interview he said goodbye. As he was leaving he said the story should be in the Sunday newspaper the following week. I said, "You should bury the story way in the back somewhere!" He turned around, lifted up his sunglasses to look me straight in the eye, and replied, "I don't think so."

 I didn't think much about the newspaper story. I'd already been interviewed by several news people by this time. But on Sunday morning, something felt different. I remember waking in my room that morning, as a very unusual quiet seemed to descend upon the city.

When I went downstairs to get the paper, I said, "Wow! What

happened?" A large picture of me was on the front page, part of a huge story that continued on many more pages. It was about more than the tragedy ... it was really about me. I didn't understand why people wanted to know more about me, as I felt this event was really about Asa.

As I surveyed the paper, I was especially glad that they had included a relatively unknown portrait of my maternal grandfather holding me shortly after my birth. I call it a portrait because Grandpa was wearing a full suit, beaming with a proud smile. He had flown over to the Big Island, the island of Hawaii, from Kauai because my mom was deeply troubled at the birth of a handicapped baby.

I was born with part of my left arm. My left arm stops a few inches below my elbow and the end of my arm looks like the early beginnings of my left hand. At that time my parents had no way of knowing about my condition until my birth. It was a great surprise, and, I imagine a very unpleasant one.

When my father came to the hospital to see me, after he checked to see that the rest of my body was okay, he simply said, "Okay. Wrap him up. We're going to take him home." I know he must have been greatly distraught, and must have had questions which could not be answered by the doctor attending my birth. But he blamed no one and nothing; he simply accepted my condition.

When my grandfather came to see me, he smiled and told my mother, "No worry! He will be alright." He said further, "Tomiko-chan, Kamisama (God) would not have given you this child unless he knew you could take care of him."

Grandpa was very old, as I remember him from a child's

perspective, and he could not speak English very well. However, this incredible act of love and encouragement for my mom was probably the greatest gift he could ever have given me as it helped her so much. We learned later that he and Grandma were some of the first Okinawans in Hawaii to convert to Christianity.

CHAPTER TWELVE

The Memorial Service

On the morning of the memorial service, which was to be held that evening, I was apprehensive as to what to expect. As the visiting hour began, the line of people waiting to see us seemed endless. It went out the door, past the driveway and onto the street of the mortuary.

My friends told me later that the people were great. They quietly shuffled along, awaiting their turn to visit our family. There were many families with children, but there was no one complaining about the long wait. They just quietly moved along in the line. Of course, earlier I had prayed earnestly for the Holy Spirit to descend and bless the entire event, including the people who were there. I am always surprised by the grace of God.

I greeted so many people my legs were giving out! I had to lean against a wall for support. I was grateful for the service to begin so I could sit down and rest. The memorial service was great. It was short and simple, about 40 minutes long. We sang "Jesus Loves Me" and "Amazing Grace." Boyden read scriptures from The Book of Ecclesiastes 3:1-8. These verses spoke that there was a time for everything. Yes, it was her time to die, hard as it was to accept. But it was her time. I had to just trust in that.

When you cannot understand what's going on, it's the one thing you can do - trust in God and Him alone. As I trust Him in all things, I cannot ever go wrong. His will is perfect and is always better than my own.

After the service, more people came to see us. It was inspiring to see so many express their condolences. Later, we packed up the leftover food and everything else. In addition to the many cards, there were stuffed animals, food and candy for the girls. I loaded up the girls in the car, who were happy and exhausted by their time outside of the main sanctuary. Thankfully, they were well occupied by the Misaki family I mentioned before.

When I got home, it took all my strength to carry the girls upstairs to bed. I passed out that night totally exhausted, but I knew I had to gear myself up for the burial to be done the next day.

The burial was actually placing Asa's cremains into a walled crypt, with those in attendance mostly close family, and friends. During the short service, I had the girls help me put Asa's urn and a few items into the wall. A man donated colored pigeons to be released. That was great. Later, I invited everyone to lunch at a banquet room at the Okinawan Cultural Center. I was very grateful that the Center opened their banquet room for our lunch as they usually do not do so on weekdays. I think they made an exception for us .

When most of the people arrived to the lunch, I thanked everyone for coming, and gave the blessing over the food. Later, everyone went home, while the girls and I returned home alone.

In the late afternoon a northerly wind blew hard into our cul-de-sac. The large monkey pod tree which sat in the middle of the cul-de-sac started releasing its leaves, and they blew directly into my garage. No matter how hard I tried to rake the leaves, more just kept on coming in. Finally, I gave up and let it come.

The entire floor of the garage was covered with the tree leaves. I remembered how Asa would always tease me for constantly sweeping the garage floor. I thought it would be her last laugh before her spirit went to heaven. The garage never got filled with leaves like that ever again.

I guess I'm like my dad who always liked his garage floor clean. He swept it constantly. But, for this day, I would wait until tomorrow to sweep the floor. It was nice to be alone with the girls that afternoon and evening, ready to carry on our lives as best as we could without Asa. The four-legged table was now ready to become one with three.

CHAPTER THIRTEEN

Church Support

Various church people came to our support. We had friends from our former church Nu'uanu Congregational Church visit us the day after the tragedy. Their hearts were breaking because they knew Asa so well. When we left this church some years ago it was hard for Asa to leave because of the strong friendships she had there.

Our Pastor at that time, Eric Ebisu, along with Associate Pastor, Keith Young, came Sunday afternoon after that fateful Friday to talk with and pray for us. It was Pastor Eric who officiated the memorial service. He has since left Pearl City Community Church and is now a missionary along with his wife Rita in Yokohama, Japan. We remain close brothers in Christ. He is the one man who I really admire who walks the talk of the Christian life.

When I returned to church services on the second Sunday after the tragedy, Pastor Keith, who led the service, noticed me in attendance. He held an impromptu prayer for me at the end of it, calling on members to lay their hand on me, or to extend their hands toward me. That congregation's prayer strengthened my spirit.

My Sunday school assistant, Owen Kawamoto, took over my 5th and 6th grade class for two Sundays before I felt okay enough to return to my teaching duties. Owen had always worked alongside me, and I am grateful for his help. A support group within the church took a collection on my behalf and was willing to help me financially in the long-term. I gratefully declined their assistance, since I felt secure in that area. I take this opportunity to thank Pearl City Community Church for their gracious support, and for so many unseen acts of kindness in the aftermath of our tragedy.

On the third Sunday after the tragedy, I decided to take the girls to the annual church camp held in Mokuleia. When we got there, our church family was ready to help us unload and set up our tent, always offering to help us in any way. I know they were very cognizant of our loss, so they were especially helpful. We had a great time at the camp which included a crab hunt, snacking on s'mores, hot dogs and shaved ice.

In addition to all the fun, something amazing happened on Sunday morning of the camp. I woke up early that morning, before sunrise and before anyone else. I had a vision as I overlooked the campgrounds sipping my coffee. I saw myself rising out of a deep well...a well that at one time was so deep that when I looked up all I could see was a glimmer of light at the top. While in this well I felt like I was holding on to, and somehow being held by a thread, one that reached to the top of the well. It was only this thin thread that held me up and kept me from falling.

Now, you can imagine how precarious my life seemed as it appeared to be hanging by a thread - one single, solitary thread. But, every day I continued to trust in God, I felt another thread come down to me, which would join the others, making that line stronger and thicker. With each passing day I was slowly being pulled up to the top of the well.

The light at the top got brighter and brighter so I knew I was moving upwards, away from the bottom of this well, up to the top. I came to understand that this thread was really my growing faith in God as He helped us through each day. With each day, my faith in God grew stronger and stronger. At the end of this vision I climbed out of the well. I was overwhelmed with joy! I was now in the light!

Finally, I realized that it was a vision that God had given me since the first day of our loss. It was telling me to *literally* "hang in there"! Telling me to just trust in Him, and that everything was going to be alright. I was overwhelmed with joy that morning, knowing that in spite of what happened, the girls and I were going to claim victory over this tragedy.

This revelation happened on the third Sunday following the tragedy. It was like our life was in a tomb for three days, only to be freed from darkness and resurrected by the Holy Spirit, like our Lord Jesus, to a new life. It was an amazing day of the amazing Lord, praise God. But it all began with my faith in God, which was hanging by a thread.

Days later, as Easter was approaching, I received a call from Pastor Elwin Ahu from New Hope Church. He asked if I would come to their Good Friday service. We later met in his church office to discuss my participation in the service. I accepted the invitation, but he warned me that the service would be located at the Neal Blaisdell Arena. They were expecting a lot of people to attend. I hesitated, but he assured me that he just wanted to call me to the stage to simply share one thing that got me through the tragedy. I simply said, "Ok."

When that evening service came, as he prompted me with the

question, I responded by saying,. "The one thing that I did was to *just hang on* to God, and never, never, never let go." But going back to our meeting when he asked me how I was doing, I told him that I felt like my life was hanging by a thread. He looked at me and said, "Did you know that Chinese silk is known to be very strong and that a single thread can hold a lot of weight?" I shook my head, but thought, "I really hope that this thread I am hanging onto is like Chinese silk... because it's all that I've got!" I am glad my girls are from China.

I am glad I did hang on to God! This means to trust Him, no matter what happens or what happened. Trust Him in all matters, even when there is no way you can understand what is going on. In the Bible, in the book of Deuteronomy, Moses repeats himself as he implores the Israelites to cling to God. I know now why he did that. The girls and I continue to trust in God and it has made all the difference in the world.

CHAPTER FOURTEEN

Gifts

After the memorial service, I came to experience the outpouring of sympathy through prayers, acts, and gifts. There was so much! I know I cannot account for all of them, especially since many were made anonymously. However, I take the opportunity now, at this writing, to express a sincere and warm appreciation to so many people who gave in so many ways.

The parent of one of Tori's soccer teammates opened a bank account for anyone to be able to donate money. As I already mentioned, when we came home from the service we brought home many books, stuffed animals, and all kinds of things for the girls. There were so many gifts to acknowledge and thank-you cards to sign; yet, I knew I could not thank everyone.

Some of the monetary gifts were sizable and were added to the girls' college funds. Regardless, I would like to mention in detail two gifts that were incredibly touching. They really grew my faith by the compassion people have for one another.

A week and a half after the tragedy, I received a phone call at about 10:00 p.m. one evening. I had been on the phone most of the time, but I was willing to take one more call. After introducing himself, the man on the line asked if he could make a surfboard for me. Surprised, and maybe a little shocked, at first I declined, saying that I don't surf. Quickly, he offered the surfboard to the girls. I also declined on their behalf, since they had not even come close to surfing yet.

Before I said goodbye and thanked him for his generous offer, I asked for his phone number just in case I changed my mind.

After I hung up the phone, I told my family and friends about the call, because I thought the idea of getting a surfboard was somewhat unusual. My friend Tim De Mello, who was there at that moment, thought I should accept the surfboard since it was a gift. After all, a gift is a gift and it should be received in gratitude.

I thought about it for a while. A few days later, I called the man up and told him that if he was still offering the surfboard, I would gladly accept it. He seemed eager to make the board for me, and immediately asked me for my measurements, both height and weight. He decided that an eight-footer would be the right size for me. He went on to say that it would take a few months to complete the board and that he would call me when it was done for me to pick it up. I said okay and waited.

Sure enough, by summer it was done, and he called me to come get the board. In anticipation of receiving it, I had bought surfboard racks for my Camry. I discovered that he actually lived near my aunt in Kaneohe. The day I went to his home, I brought two cases of good beer to thank him; unfortunately, since he did not drink alcohol, it took some encouragement on my part for him to accept it. My gift of beer was dumb, I know now. I assumed that since he was a surfer he would surely drink beer.

Anyway, when I got there he proudly showed me the board, and it was a beauty, too...brand new and glossy, colored white with blue and green graphics. It took a while before I could give the board a try, but I found it was very challenging, since paddling with one arm makes me go in circles.

After that one failed attempt at surfing, I needed to rethink how I was going to use the surfboard. Even if I were able to paddle to catch a wave, standing up with one arm is really difficult since it usually takes two hands to hold the board steady to jump on it. I thought it was impossible until I saw the movie *Soul Surfer*, where Brittany Hamilton, in a split moment, pushes herself up on the board with one hand.

Later, with surf sessions provided as a gift from a family member, the girls and I actually learned how to surf off Waikiki. We were taught by legendary surfer Dane Kealoha who was very patient and kind. He kept working with us until all of us got up on the board and surfed at least one wave.

But seeing that we were not using the board, and it was just stored in the garage, I decided to donate it to a program called "Kids Hurt, Too". This program provides group therapy to children who have lost a parent or close family member. My girls participated in the grief program for a year and I think it really helped them deal with their own loss. Within that program is an activity called *Surfing For the Soul*. In this activity, experienced adult surfers take children out to surf the calm waves at Waikiki Beach and teach children who have experienced great loss how to surf. I thank Jon B. Mar for this most wonderful, heartfelt gift of a beautiful, brand new surfboard that now has a good purpose, and a worthy home.

The second gift I would like to make note of was from a total stranger, one who doesn't even reside in Hawaii. About a month after the tragedy, I got a phone call from a man asking if I was the person involved in it. He then explained that he was a total stranger, one that just happened to be on vacation in Hawaii when the event occurred. He said he didn't know what he would do, but that he would like to help me somehow. He asked me if the girls and I would meet him and his wife over lunch. I will call him Jim for the story.

We arranged to meet at a local eatery and Jim's wife graciously brought gift bags for the girls filled with toys and treats. At the end of our lunch I thanked him for his time, and told him that he was not obligated to do anything; rather, that having lunch together and meeting them was enough. A couple of weeks later, Jim called. He asked if it was okay if he could create college accounts for the girls. I said yes, so he said he would have his attorney contact me later on the details.

About a month after that I got an email from his attorney. This email informed me that Jim would open college accounts in amounts that would greatly assure their college education. I nearly fell out of my chair at the email message. How incredibly generous was this gift, and from a total stranger no less!

Over the years I would send letters to Jim along with the girls' school pictures, updating him about their progress in school, and in life in general. Needless to say, Jim has become Uncle Jim in our household!

Their college education was made secure by this, together with the funds many others have given the girls. It was so wonderful to be able to tell them that their college education was paid for. I don't think they quite understood what college was about, since they were so young, but I knew. The generosity of people through this tragedy had greatly uplifted my spirit and that of the girls. God's love and grace is truly amazing.

CHAPTER FIFTEEN

Along Came A Man Named John

At some point during the weeks following the tragedy, a woman from our church approached me to see if I wanted to talk to a man who had some information about Asa's death. At first I had no interest in talking to this person, because I was just trying to survive day by day, if not moment by moment. Asa was gone, and nothing was going to change that.

After a while, though, I began to wonder what she had gone through during the attack. It was my greatest hope that she died quickly, and somehow was not in great pain or suffering. I was hoping that the workers in the nail shop at which she sought refuge would have helped her. Later, after talking with the owner, I came to the understanding that they did not touch her, only stared at her condition while she was on the floor. They also took pictures of her which they offered to show me but I declined. I think it's a cultural practice of some people to take pictures of the deceased to share them with others.

The question still remained: what was she going through? Was she possibly dying by herself with no one to care for her?

Once again, I was told that this man would like to offer information about that day. This time I accepted the offer, hoping I could get answers to my questions. I was given his name and his phone number. His name was John. He happened to be the boyfriend of a woman who worked as a caregiver of a family member of the woman that approached me from my church.

I called him on a weekend and introduced myself. He seemed excited to get my call. He went on to explain that he came upon the scene soon after Asa was attacked, while she lay dying in a pool of her blood. The attacker had already left the immediate area. John just happened to be exercising, walking through the shopping center when he came upon the scene with Asa on the floor. John, being a cardiac nurse, immediately came to Asa's aid, holding her in his arms, providing pressure to her wounds, gently speaking to her to hold on until the ambulance arrived.

As he spoke about what happened, I could not believe my ears! Here was someone, a total stranger, who came to Asa's aid in her last moments of life. Would my questions finally be answered?

I carefully asked him, "What was her countenance in the aftermath of the attack? What was she like at this time? Was she in obvious pain? Was she suffering terribly?" John said, "No. She was resting, taking comfortable breaths as she lay on my lap."

He gave me so much comfort and peace, to know that someone provided care and love - yes love - to my beloved wife. His voice started to crack as he confessed how he felt so guilty that he could not do anything more to help her. I said, "John, you did everything that was possible! You did all that I could ever wish for."

This was true, because just that week I had been told by my neighbor - who happened to be the supervising nurse at the hospital - that she had read the medical records of that day. She saw that Asa's main arteries were cut so deeply that there was no way she could have survived.

At the moment I told him this, I could feel the weight of guilt release from John's shoulders as he heard the truth he needed to hear. Suddenly our conversation became very light as we talked about the possibility of meeting face-to-face. A week or so later John and his fiancée came over to my home to have ice cream dessert with me and the girls. This meeting allowed me to thank him personally for all that he had done for Asa.

That evening I told John that I believed God used him on that day to bring comfort and care to Asa when neither I, nor anyone else, could. Praise God for His peace that surpasses understanding.

CHAPTER SIXTEEN

Bringing Back Some Normalcy For The Girls

It was the third week since the tragedy and after keeping the girls home for a week, then bringing them back to soccer the second week, I decided it was time for them to go back to school. I sensed I needed to talk to the girls about what happened so that they would have the story straight, because I know there were all kinds of rumors swirling about what happened. I was amazed to find out that Tori thought Asa was shot by a gun. I guess with all that was going around, the important facts were lost on the girls.

So, I sat them down and explained as honestly and simply as I could about what happened. I said mom was eating saimin outside of the shaved ice store at the Ewa Town Center when suddenly a stranger attacked her with a knife, and stabbed her in the chest. She was later taken to the hospital which was right across from our subdivision, where she died from her wounds. They listened to me intently and did not ask any questions. I said, "Now, you got the story straight. So, if anyone talks to you about it, you can say 'yes' that happened or 'no', it did not. Kids will talk, that's what they do.

I am very grateful to Katie's school counselor, who provided grief counseling for her. She could also share her experience with a classmate who lost her father about a year earlier. Moreover, I am also very grateful to the support of the school through the principal, teachers, and staff for all the years that the girls attended Holomua Elementary.

Principal Norman Pang was especially helpful defending Asa after the tragedy. There was talk that Asa cut out of work early, and should not have been at the shopping center at the time of the attack. The truth was shared by Principal Pang in a letter that was published by the newspaper. It said that she took a leave day to chaperone and assist in a long time fundraising event at the school. She later planned to go to the shopping center to see our dentist and get a haircut.

When her car did not start that morning at the school, she called me to ask me what to do. That's when I told her to just walk to the shopping center and wait until I could get there, and then we would pick up the girls. But, then, some plans don't go as planned.

When I dropped Tori off at her preschool classroom on the first day she came back, I noticed a fellow student smiling at us, seemingly happy to see Tori was back. It was obvious he wanted to engage in conversation with her. After signing her in, I bent down and spoke to her saying, "Remember, you know the truth about what happened. If anyone says anything otherwise, just say that it is not true, and tell them what really happened." She looked at me and nodded her head.

At the end of the day, after I signed her out, I asked her if any kid talked to her about what happened. She said, "Yes, and I told them the truth." I smiled and said, "Yes, the truth is the truth."

Both of the girls seemed to be doing pretty well back in school. At least their teachers did not notice any outward difficulties. Only the Lord knows what was really happening inside of their hearts. Truly, I am grateful that I can trust in that. I can only imagine how tough it was for them. At the time of Asa's death, Tori was four years old and Katie was seven.

CHAPTER SEVENTEEN

My Going Back To Work

It was also good for me to go back to school, and work, as it brought more normalcy to my life. Some people seemed surprised at my return, thinking I was better off taking off the rest of the year. But it was good to be back to finish the year.

Most of my students were happy to see me. Some shared how they could not believe what happened. I responded that the whole experience did not seem real to me either. I remember telling one class that I felt as though I went through a fire and that my entire body had been refined, like forged metal.

The next school year was better for me since both girls were at the same school. Tori was starting kindergarten and Katie was in the third grade. That was the year the school week was reduced to 4 days because of a budget saving furlough program called "Furlough Fridays". This resulted in an across-the-board 5% pay cut for teachers. I was actually glad since it gave me more time to spend with the girls. But it was a hard time for many Hawaii residents and families who suffered long periods of unemployment due to the Recession of 2008.

CHAPTER EIGHTEEN

On Single Parenting

On the morning after our tragedy, when I got off the floor after the Lord spoke to me saying, "You CAN" (take care of the girls), I did not really know how I was going to do it. I just knew that God gave me the confidence to take on the challenge. God has been with me every step of the way, but that is not to say it was *easy*.

Man, it was *hard*, really hard at times. I soon realized that I had to do it my way, as best as I knew how; that I would do things differently than Asa, probably way worse than she, but still, I needed to get the job done.

I shared earlier how the girls complained that I was not gentle when washing their hair. My reply was that I just get the job done, like washing my car. Besides, I didn't have the luxury of having a partner to assist me as a parenting couple would. Typically, a parenting couple could share family and household duties, but now as a single parent, I got double to do and less time to do things. But I did the best I could... which I believe is all that the Lord wanted from me.

I must admit I tried my best to do it *all*, which was probably not realistic. I tried my best to maintain the lifestyle we had before. This meant other than school, the girls would keep their extracurricular activities of soccer and gymnastics. I helped coach and referee all of their soccer teams, which usually meant rushing home after school and work to get to practice, then get home to quickly cook dinner, bathe the girls and put them to bed. I was usually exhausted each night by 9:30 p.m. and enjoyed an hour of rest before going to bed - if I didn't have shopping or grading assignments to do. When I looked back at all I did, I don't know how I did it ... except I know that the Lord gave me strength. The girls probably learned a lot about patience, and I guess patience is not a bad thing to learn.

So it was hard at times. I must admit, and confess, that at times I started to notice that I would get angry and yell at the girls at the top of my lungs for something they did. God only knows how angry I got. Poor Tori was clumsy at times, and her spilling food on the table or carpet usually got me going. I would start yelling and poor Katie would just freeze. I knew I was terribly wrong to yell at them, but sometimes the pressure of trying to get everything done and on time was too much.

Regardless, I knew that the yelling had to stop. I could not do this by my own effort, which of course meant I had to confess and pray to God for help. As I started to pray about this matter, I began to catch myself before I said anything, and just made myself walk away to cool off. It also meant I had to apologize to the girls for the yelling and ask for their forgiveness.

I decided that I had to stop caring about anything that was getting me angry. I determined to commit myself to being calm with the girls, even when they gave me real cause to raise my anger level and my voice, because yelling is simply not acceptable. Being calm even when I was angry was not easy. But with God all things are possible and doable.

In one of my prayer groups I confessed that I needed to stop yelling at the girls. Suddenly almost every guy in the room confessed that they did the same thing to their kids. It's not an easy thing to share but it's good to get it out there in the open and have others pray for you, and for themselves, too. By the way, this is what prayer groups are for. If you or your group members cannot be honest and share real stuff about life, God will not come in to help.

Some experiences of my single parenting were funny - or not - depending on your perspective. Among the many gifts the girls received in the aftermath of our tragedy were bath and skin products. At some point the girls had received several bottles of lotions, soaps, and *body wash*. I had no idea what body wash was and that it was actually a soap.

I saw a TV commercial that looked like it was applied to your skin after you bathe, like skin lotion. One time when Tori asked for lotion for her dry skin I just gave her a bottle of body wash, thinking it was the same as skin lotion. Boy, was I wrong. One day, after using some body wash for a week, she started complaining that her skin on her legs was peeling. I told her that she should just use more.

Finally, she adamantly told me that body wash cannot be the same as skin lotion. This is one of those many times I could have used some female help, but like I said, I did the best I could. I know, I should have asked for help. But remember, I am a guy. Still, I did the best I could do for the girls.

This leads to my most important point about single parenting, and it's specifically directed to fathers who lose their wives, for whatever reason. It is this: do not give up your children to another relative or entity to care for them. It's good to use their help, but really bad to give them away. Over the years I've heard stories of fathers doing this. While, on the surface, it seems logical to send your children away since many men are clueless about how to take care of the physical part of their children' needs. But like anything else, you can learn anything, as long as you're willing.

You will make mistakes - I've made a ton of them - but you make less of them over time, and soon you'll get the hang of things. You may never be as good as your wife in washing or drying their hair, but what the kids need more than perfect parenting is *You*. What they need most is you as their father; for you to never give up, and never give them up.

Don't worry about making things perfect, which even your wife could not really do. The greatest gifts are lessons you are teaching them by keeping them in your care: persistence and perseverance, not to mention flexibility and adaptability.

What parent would not want their children to learn and develop these character traits?

How can children learn these important character traits if you don't use this solemn opportunity to demonstrate and model these traits for them. In fact, I believe you teach them just the opposite of these traits if you simply give them up and give up your fatherhood.

I say NEVER, NEVER, NEVER give up on your daddy card. It's the most important card you need to play in your family life. This was also an opportunity to truly live my faith in God. If God is real, and His promises are true, then our new life situation has to work out for good. And our life has worked out for good, in more ways than you, or even I, will ever know.

If you want to know how faithful God is then put your faith in Him. If you want your children to develop faith in God, let them see your faith in Him, because the Bible says it is faith that pleases God. (Hebrews 11:6) And from his pleasure, he will bless, provide, guide, and protect you and your family.

Honestly, I would like to think that I would have kept the girls without God speaking to me on that kitchen floor. But when I think about it, if I was going to keep the girls, then why did God have to speak to me? Just like the good Father He is, the Lord comes in when we need him most and for that we must live to give Him all the glory. Amen.

*Asa at her desk at Waianae High School.
Photo featured on her memorial service program.*

The trio: Asa, Tori, and Katie having fun in the rare rain downpours in Ewa Beach.

The two girls: Katie (5) reading to Tori (2) before bedtime.

FORGIVENESS AND FAITH

BRYAN I. YAMASHITA

CHAPTER NINETEEN

FORGIVENESS

I think it's a little amusing that when I thought I was close to completing this book I suddenly realized I had not written about forgiveness. Forgiveness is actually a large part of my story. I'm not sure how I forgot about this, but I think because of our timely forgiveness for Asa's killer, the girls and I have been able to move on much better with our lives without the burden of anger and resentment. This, in turn, allowed us to leave behind much of our pain, thereby leading us to almost forgetting our act of forgiveness.

First of all, I need to say, I was not a very forgiving guy. Forgiveness was one of the biggest issues between my mom and dad. He had a hard time saying "sorry", so I did not learn much about repentance from him. For much of his life he was a very good man and took pride in that, but when it came time to say sorry, he just couldn't say it.

Thankfully, my mom tried to drill that word into me, but like I said, I was still not a forgiving guy. I guess for much of my life I had more of an Old Testament view, with "an eye for an eye." If you cut me off on the road I could quickly imagine calling on an F-15 air strike to blast your car straight to heaven or somewhere else.

Before I could forgive Asa's killer, I needed to learn about, and practice, forgiveness myself. It began for me at Pearl City Community Church when I was serving as a teacher in the summer school program in 2008 in the children's ministry. I remember I noted on a poster board the scripture that was the basis for that summer's program. It came from Deuteronomy 31:6, which said, "The Lord Your God will go with you. He will never leave or forsake you." This scripture alone has been a powerful rock during our loss which has sustained us in so many ways.

Anyway, the Sunday School director, Rita Ebisu, wife of Pastor Eric, somehow saw some teaching potential in me. I've taught high school social studies during my entire teaching career, so I guess it made sense that I could take on a bunch of fifth and sixth graders for a change on Sundays.

Things were going pretty well as I tackled Sunday morning lessons with about ten kids who usually came to class. Teaching Sunday school is challenging, because you have little leverage in the classroom, unlike a regular teacher in school. Besides, who can blame kids for any misbehavior when they have been in regular school all week, and then on Sunday, they are back in Sunday school.

Along with my assistant, Owen Kawamoto, we did the best we could to teach about the incredible love and grace of Jesus Christ and our great Father in heaven. But things got rough for me when we came up on the lesson about *forgiveness*. As I planned my lesson before that Sunday morning, I became more and more apprehensive about teaching the topic. Then God revealed to me that there were people I needed to forgive before I could teach my children about forgiveness on that Sunday. Of course, it would be hypocritical to teach on the topic if I myself did not forgive others for their offenses against me.

I thought hard and long. Finally, I remembered two people, in two separate work situations, that I needed to forgive. I believe to this day that in both cases, both offenders purposely, for reasons I cannot imagine, were out to make my life miserable. If I had to guess, their actions against me were due to professional jealousy. Although these cases happened long ago, whenever I remembered them, I would get angry quickly. I can honestly say that if I saw these people cross the street in front of my car, I would not hesitate to run them over, truly.

Regardless, I needed to forgive them, although I didn't want to. I had to forgive them otherwise my lesson on Sunday would be nothing but a lie. Finally, I went to God in prayer and said, "God, You have got to help me forgive these people or I cannot teach this lesson." By Saturday night, the weight of unforgiveness was so heavy on my heart I started scrambling to find another lesson for the next day.

On Sunday morning, I woke up feeling lighter, like a weight was lifted off my shoulders and chest. I went into prayer and checked my heart and yes, I had forgiven these people. My heart was clean! Now, thinking about these people brought no more darkness, but rather a new compassion for them, with best wishes for them wherever they were. I guess my one regret is that it took teaching Sunday School many years later to practice forgiveness in my own life. I guess it's like raising children: when a difficult situation arises, they will bring to light the deficiencies of our character.

Hurray! I was now ready to teach about forgiveness. My lesson went well. I could speak with conviction about the need to forgive others and look my students in their eyes. I recall our lesson focused on Psalm 91 and Acts 7. This Psalm speaks of

God's protection over us against evil. Acts 7 was about the trial of Steven, with him being stoned to death.

I asked my students how God could speak of His holy protection, and yet allow His servant Steven to get stoned to death. I myself could not explain this apparent difference in the scriptures. So, I decided to simply present it to my students and to hear what they thought. They were quiet for a while and then I asked them, "Can you still trust God even when you are being attacked?" As they kept their gaze down, slowly one by one, each nodded in agreement that they would trust God even during great trial.

I smiled and thought, yes, we do need to be like children to gain salvation, to trust like they do. On that day, the tables were turned, the students taught the teacher an important lesson. Trusting in God empowers us to choose to forgive and love others. Amen.

It was not long after that Sunday school lesson that we experienced our family's tragedy, and I publicly spoke about forgiveness, and my need to forgive Asa's killer. The truth was that I did not really forgive him. I felt like I did, because I had no anger against him, and this in itself seemed remarkable. So much so that my friend Tim came back to my home for two days after the tragedy to make sure my calm composure was real, and that I wasn't really steaming with anger.

So why did I not experience anger over such an offensive event? Well, on one level, as I explained earlier, I was not angry for what he did. It was an unwarranted attack, and though so very violent and severe, simply did not make sense to me. Because it made no sense, I simply could not get angry over that.

On a spiritual level, I realized that I was covered by God's grace on that day because my heart was cleansed by forgiving others in my past. I think the Old Testament speaks of this same covering over the Israelites when they sacrificed animals to God for the forgiveness of their sins. But this covering was partial and temporary; it had to be repeated each year.

Therefore forgiveness would not be complete until the ultimate acceptance of the sacrifice of Jesus on the cross and the cleansing of all our sins by a one-time shedding of his blood. This offer of salvation was and is freely given for our sins. Its only requirement is for us to repent and ask God for forgiveness.

However, my covering was temporary as well. I remember sharing my testimony at my church. When asked by my pastor about how I was able to forgive the killer, I simply responded, "It was God's grace," which it truly was. My forgiveness began with God's covering of my heart but this was temporary and I still needed to actually forgive him.

It was not until I was back at work that I was confronted by the Lord while driving to and from work. It was on these drives that I would pray and talk with God a lot. On one drive the Lord asked me, "Did you forgive him?" I remember I did not quickly respond, because after everything that happened so far, I realized I really did not forgive the killer. Then I asked God, "Do I really have to forgive him? After all, I don't hate him, and that should be good enough," but the Lord said, "Yes."

"How can I forgive him for what he did?" I retorted. "Wasn't it so terrible?" The Lord became quiet. After a while I said, "Oh God... I cannot forgive him on my own, by my own power. You have to help me. Can You help me forgive him? Please Lord, help me forgive him, I cannot do this on my own."

A few days later, as I was driving to work, I thought again about forgiving Asa's killer. I felt a heavy burden lifted off my shoulders and an incredible lightness throughout my body and soul. That's when I realized I had truly forgiven this man. I was filled with great joy, knowing I was truly released from the burden of unforgiveness.

Then I began to wonder, did I really forgive him? So I asked God, "How do I know if I really forgave the Killer?" The Lord said, "Love him." But I said, "How can I love him?" Then I knew what I had to do. I began to pray for this man, pray for God to bless him wherever he was, to bless him with whatever he needed. I even thought of testing my forgiveness by visualizing the killer in the best place he could be. I actually visualized him in an expensive Waikiki Resort enjoying himself with all the amenities the resort had to offer. As I had this thought I responded by thinking that if that's where God wants him to be, that is sufficient for me.

Now, I am truly free of the burden of unforgiveness, and of its burden of anger and resentment. Because I forgave him, I have peace; the peace of Christ Jesus which surpasses all understanding. Amen.

Before school ended that year, I was approached by a representative of a non-affiliated religious organization called the Forgiveness Project. This man asked me if I would receive one of the forgiveness awards given at their yearly meeting sometime during the summer. I accepted the invitation to receive this award and was honored along with two other recipients. I can't remember what I said in my acceptance speech, but it was good to know that forgiveness is important in many religions.

More importantly, I remembered that I realized that my act of forgiveness was not only important for my well-being, but it was much more important for my girls to forgive as well. As the other award recipients spoke to the audience I noticed my girls were in front of me on the floor below the stage, playing with their toys. As I watched them play quietly, I realized that my life is short but they have a whole lifetime to live, and that unforgiveness would be a far greater burden if they had to carry it throughout their whole lives. It was at that point that I realized that the girls need to forgive their mother's killer, too.

By the end of spring of 2010 my family had left Pearl City Community Church and we were visiting other churches to attend. As we visited other church services, the girls attended whatever Sunday school programs that were offered. One night as I was putting the girls to bed, Tori turned to Katie and asked, "What does seventy times seven equal?" Now I know Katie knew mathematically the answer to that question but what I didn't understand was why Tori was asking Katie this question. Again, Tori asked Katie the question. This time Katie was upset and yelled back, "490!" I calmed the girls down, we prayed together and I left the room wondering what that was all about.

While downstairs on the couch I realized Tori's question was based on the scripture from Matthew 18:22, which explains how Jesus says we must forgive others and do so unceasingly. I sensed Tori was really asking Katie if she had forgiven their mom's killer. Then I remembered that the girls needed to forgive the man as well as I did.

The next day at dinner I talked to the girls about forgiveness and their need to forgive the man who killed their mother. I asked them if they would forgive him for what he did. After a short moment, they both said, "Yes, we forgive him."

I was incredibly overjoyed by their response and thanked them for their action. To mark this momentous event I had the girls write a statement of forgiveness in their own handwriting and spelling. The girls forgave the killer on June 21, 2010. I had their papers posted on our foyer wall to honor their act of faith.

The girls told me later that the topic of forgiveness came up in a Sunday school lesson they received while we visited New Hope Kapolei. The following Sunday we returned to the church and I personally thanked their Sunday School teachers for their part in helping the girls forgive others. This act of forgiveness led us to our own baptism, all three of us, on July 4th, 2010 at Grace Bible Church Kapolei. I am so proud of Katie and Tori for taking this step of faith and their obedience to God and Christ Jesus!

As mentioned before, the name of Asa's killer is Tittleman Fauatea. His trial for the murder of Asa took place in 2013, about four years after the crime. Yes, the wheels of justice move pretty slowly. Before the trial he was held in prison. I was notified by the prosecuting attorney that I had to testify at the trial. I was called to testify to simply state that Asa was my wife and that she was at the shopping center on that day, after which I was excused. I didn't stay for the rest of the trial because it didn't matter much to me. It was up to the court to decide his fate. Again, Asa was gone and nothing was going to bring her back.

After the trial he was found guilty for murder in the second degree. He was sentenced to life in prison. Later the parole board reduced his sentence to around sixty years with a chance of parole. On his sentencing date I was given an opportunity to be present and speak in court. When the judge called me up to give me a chance to address the court, it felt strange to be just several feet from the person who committed such a violent act against my family. This was my one chance I could speak directly to the killer and I was ready to say what I needed to say.

After thanking the court for their work in this case and the chance to speak, I turned to the killer and said, "Mr. Fauatea, my daughters and I forgive you for killing our wife and mother." In that moment the court seemed calm, as many people knew that I had already extended forgiveness to this man. Then I said what I felt was equally, if not more, important for him. I said, "But what you need to do is confess to God for what you have done." In that moment I felt the atmosphere of the court change suddenly as it seemed the judge spoke to cut off my speech. I think it was because I used the word "confess", which means in a court of law an admission of guilt for a crime. But I was speaking about the confession of sin to God.

As I sat back down I was grateful I got to say what I needed to say. In that moment I became more concerned about his salvation; that all of us, including Mr. Fauatea, need to repent of our sins and turn to God, no matter what sins we have committed in our lives. Now, not only do the girls and I forgo any claim against him, we are now concerned for his salvation, which is up to him. The Lord gave us free choice. Adam chose to sin against God's command, but all of us have the choice to repent, turn around, and walk with Jesus as our Lord and savior.

My time in that courtroom was short but I'd like to believe it was significant. Praise God for his forgiveness and offer of salvation.

CHAPTER TWENTY

What Is Forgiveness?

First, because there are so many ideas about forgiveness, let's discuss what it is *not*.

Forgiveness is not forgetting the offense! You will probably always remember a very bad offense. It's like a scar from a terrible wound. Overtime the wound heals, but the scar will always remain.

Forgiveness has nothing to do with anything about what the offender needs to do to make up for the offense. In other words, it's not about the offender apologizing and saying sorry, or doing any kind of penance. It would be great if there was an honest, heartfelt apology by the offender which, upon its acceptance, can lead to reconciliation.

Forgiveness is not about any of these things. If there were some kind of penance to be served, who would decide on it? You, the offended person? The offended person cannot really decide on the penance. For in addition to any offense, what can satisfy a broken ego or hurt pride? Nothing can really satisfy the offended person's insatiable demands.

There would be no end to the penance. Only God can decide any punishment or verdict because only God sees everything and knows everything. It's only God's court that matters. It is written in the scriptures, "Vengeance is mine" (Deuteronomy 32:35) This is why we are not to judge. We cannot fully judge fairly because we don't have all the information.

With two eyes we actually see very little and therefore understand very little. No matter what any court of law on this Earth does, a truly righteous judgement is impossible. Only God can rule or judge righteously, because again, only he sees everything and knows everything.

So what is forgiveness? Merriam Webster's dictionary says *forgiveness* is to give up resentment of, or claim to, any requital for compensation or retaliation. To forgive means to cease to feel any resentment against the offender. Again, in other words, it is all about what you need to do, the one offended -- not about the offender.

So must we forgive others? The Bible says we must forgive in order to be forgiven. We need to be forgiven because of the sins we commit. Therefore, we must forgive. But this is not for God's benefit, this is for our benefit. When we forgive others we release all anger and resentment against the offender. It is a burden of which we let go; this makes us free to love and care for others, as God wants us to. It lets us live in His kingdom of peace, hope and love.

If we do not forgive, we keep carrying our anger, resentment or bitterness. None of these bring peace, hope, love and joy. Unforgiveness cannot coexist or be compatible with the fruits of the Holy Spirit. Unforgiveness is incompatible with the presence of God and His amazing grace. This is why he requires us to forgive, because he wants us to be with Him. If we do not forgive, we cannot enter his glory.

So how do we forgive? Forgiveness first begins with a choice. God gave us free will so we must choose to forgive. We also forgive out of obedience to God's command. But how do we do something that is seemingly impossible for so many of us? We forgive not by our power but through the help of God's power. We can ask in prayer for God to help us forgive.

Be in daily and constant prayer, humbling ourselves, knowing we are only dust and God has all the glory and the power. God will help you because he loves us, and therefore wants the best for us. Though forgiving others can seem impossible, with God all things are possible (Matthew 19:26). I am amazed that we, as Christians, ask God for many things but do not ask for help in the most difficult areas of our lives, especially, this area of unforgiveness. So please ask, the good Lord wants to help us. I did, and He surely helped me.

I believe the following scriptures support my ideas about forgiveness:

Matthew 6:14 **"If you forgive those who sin against you, your heavenly father will forgive you. But if you refuse to forgive others, your father will not forgive your sins."**

Matthew 11:25 **"But when you are praying, first forgive anyone you are holding a grudge against, so that your father in heaven will forgive your sins too."** Notice the scripture implies that forgiveness should be done soon, not to be procrastinated about or slowed.

Matthew 18:21-35 This is about the parable of the unforgiving debtor. If you do not forgive, the father will not forgive you; and therefore, because the father forgives, we must have mercy and forgive others.

Luke 6:37 **"Do not judge others, and you will not be**

judged. Do not condemn others, or it will all come back against you. Forgive others, and you will be forgiven."

Matthew 6:12 **"...and forgive us for our sins, as we have forgiven those who sin against us."** (The Lord's prayer) The Lord's forgiveness of our sins is based upon our forgiveness of others.

CHAPTER TWENTY ONE

Summer Of 2009

I was so looking forward to the summer: a time to rest and spend time with the girls, to have fun, and enjoy each other's company. What followed was not what I was expecting.

In June, on Katie's first day of summer vacation, she was in the car complaining that her heart was beating rapidly. I rushed her to the hospital, where her heart beat normalized. Her doctor decided to have her wear a heart monitor twenty-four hours a day for a month. Oh joy, what a start to our vacation.

I took some time to clean out some of Asa's stuff at home, work stuff that she obviously would not be needing, and storing some personal belongings in the house attic. Then came sickness. Somehow we all got sick, a total of four colds during the summer ending with H1N1 that brought a fever as high as 108 for Katie. Man, I thought I was going to lose her. The girls' doctor could not believe how often during that summer we went to see him. You could see it in his face as he kept asking us, "Again?" I would simply look back at him and say, "Yes, again."

As for me, I had a low-grade fever throughout the whole summer. I would wake up in the morning with the fever and it would stay with me throughout the whole day. As I fell into my slumber every evening, the fever remained. It was not until the first day of classes back at school that I my fever finally broke. I finally broke free from the fever but not until I had to get back to work. What luck. I wonder if it was demonic. I never experienced a sickness like that one, which lasted for so long. Gratefully, I never broke free from God as he kept us together through it all.

CHAPTER TWENTY TWO

The Meaning Of Sacrifice

I think it was during that summer after the tragedy that I had a somewhat strange experience. For some reason, I think it was God, I was drawn to look at one of Asa's prized possessions-a two-volume copy of The Oxford Unabridged Dictionary which has every English word in existence. It comes in two huge volumes and the print is so small that they include a magnifying glass to see the words.

I rarely open this dictionary but I was somehow drawn to it. Alone in my office I flipped through the pages and the word *sacrifice* came to my mind. Well, of course I knew what the word meant as it is commonly used: to forsake something of value for something else, hopefully something of equal value or more.

I looked up the word in the dictionary anyway to see what the book says. I was somewhat surprised to see in the definition the words: *to kill a small animal like a sheep or lamb which is perfect and clean, killed with a knife.*

Those words suddenly struck me. Asa was a small person by comparison, about four feet ten tall, and weighed about eighty-seven pounds. Before she was stabbed by the killer, she had her hair cut very short, and then had a dental teeth cleaning. In the attack she was stabbed with a very sharp new kitchen knife.

So was she some kind of sacrifice? And if she was, what was the sacrifice made for?

To this day I believe only God can answer the question as to why Asa died that day. However, I believe in a sovereign Lord above everything whose ways are not mine but are better than mine. He thinks in ways I cannot even imagine. I continue to trust in Him who is perfect and whose name is holy and above all names.

CHAPTER TWENTY THREE

Dreams and Premonitions

I believe God speaks to us in dreams and I had many about Asa's death. My brother Boyden helped me understand many of these dreams since his church specializes in dream interpretation. In most of my dreams about Asa she is dressed in a beautiful white dress with her face made up and hair perfect. She is happy and she looks stunning. This is one of the reasons I know she is in a very good place. Sometimes she just appears and I see her smiling.

In one dream she spoke to me briefly. I was in a room with a table. On the table were belts and buckles of all sorts. They were all fastened together, arranged neatly on the table. I tried to unfasten the belt buckles, moving from one to another without success. It was a little frustrating, but understandable, since I was trying to unbuckle the belts with one hand as I would in real life. It's what I would do naturally since I actually only have one hand, but I do manage to get it done.

Anyway, I was working on releasing one of the belt buckles when she came up to me out of nowhere and said, "Well, just do it and get on." When I awoke and remembered the dream, its meaning became soon apparent to me. Asa was telling me to move on with my life by unbuckling the belts of our marriage and to find another love.

This was something that I was looking forward to doing, but at a later point in time. God told me I had to wait. This is one dream where she talked to me. I don't recall having any other conversations with her in other dreams.

I recall another significant dream during this time after Asa's death. She was not in it at all. It was a dream that revealed God's promise of salvation to me.

In my dream I was hiking up a mountain where I could see a trail that crossed to another side of it. On the trail I saw people hiking up along it, going higher and higher. Then I was suddenly on top of the mountain where there was a viewing room overlooking the views from the top of the mountain. There were other people there who were enjoying the view too. We saw clouds and mist, lower ridges and other mountain tops, beautiful earthly colors of every kind. It was like a grand view of nature from the highest mountain.

I remember just being in complete bliss standing on top of that mountain. Then I was taken to a slightly lower part of the mountain, where there appeared a young man in a white robe with a sash or rope fastened around his waist. His arms were revealed and they were strong, with hands that do manual labor. I did not see his face, but I wondered if this was Jesus. Then, the dream ended.

I believe the dream allowed me to see a view of heaven and my path to heaven. More importantly, the dream allowed me to be in the presence of my Lord and Savior Jesus Christ. It is a dream that gives me hope for what I can look forward to, either when Jesus comes back to earth, or when I die and go to him. The trail symbolizes my life's journey that I must walk on, to follow God's ways, and to stay on His path. But waiting on top of that mountain, at the end of my life is paradise - heaven!

Going to a lower place on the mountain and seeing Jesus means that I still have work to do while on my path and to join Jesus in completing this work. At the end of the year after Asa's death, many of these dreams began to fade. But it really was that year that I needed God to speak to me the most and I believe he did so in my dreams.

As I wrote earlier about God separating me from Asa and preparing me for my loss I also discovered another premonition related to her death. I did not make this discovery until about a year after the tragedy.

I was cleaning my bedroom when I came across a paperback novel titled "A Prayer for Owen Meany" by John Irving. I remember Asa always keeping it by her bedside and occasionally reading it. I asked her on one occasion, "Aren't you done reading that book by now?" I asked her this because she kept it on her nightstand for years. She replied, "I finished it a long time ago but I just like reading portions of it again." She never shared what part she liked. I would just see her reading in the middle of it, skipping to another part, but always reading it.

We saw a movie made from the novel, but like most movies based on novels, it was somewhat disappointing as the movie's telling was very different from the book. I am hardly an avid reader myself, but one day I picked up the book, wondering for the first time why she liked reading it so much so I began to read it.

I was fascinated. It was a number One International Bestseller, but acclaims like that usually don't excite me. But this book did. I could hardly put it down. Sometimes I would keep reading well into the early morning hours even though I had to get up soon to go to work. The story was an amazing one about a boy who was born very small, who wondered what his purpose in life was. He knew he would do something big but he had no idea what it would be. Though challenged by his small stature, he had a booming voice, but to what purpose?

The story is told in the words of his best friend who had long doubts about himself, as well; I guess we all do. It became apparent to me as I read the book that Asa could easily relate to this character, Owen Meany, who, like him, was a very small person. Asa had great dreams and ambitions like him. She had great drive and motivation like him. And most of all, she wondered what her purpose on this earth was for.

Unfortunately, the main character Owen learns that he will die one day, not of old age as most of us look forward to, but to die prematurely, before his time. He is totally clueless about how he will die. Worse yet, he knows the exact day he will die. But when he dies, it all makes sense. Everything that happened in his life had prepared him for that fateful day.

I wonder if Asa had similar thoughts of her fate. And perhaps on her fateful day, in that moment that as she lay dying in the arms of a total stranger, everything that happened in her life made sense to her.

I was dumbfounded when I finished reading the book. I tried to share this revelation of the book to others about how the novel related to what happened to Asa but I thought it was not well received. Maybe, it was a matter of a person needing to read the book to understand any correlation.

RESTORATION AND HOPE

CHAPTER TWENTY FOUR

Getting Married Again

It was just about a month after the tragedy. The girls and I were waiting at a traffic light on our way to school when I turned to them and said, "I'm just letting you know, I want to get married again." They were both quiet at my announcement. Asa was gone. We missed her and I missed being married. I knew in my heart I had the capacity to love again.

In about a year, I decided to change churches. I decided to attend Grace Bible Kapolei out on the west side, in Makakilo. It was a small church that met at an elementary school. Its Pastor, Mike Ohara, had asked me earlier to testify and share about our tragedy at one of their services. As we attended the services, I felt that the church was a good fit for myself and the girls.

While there, the pastor's mother-in-law, Nancy Young, for a long time had run a singles- ministry out of her home, bringing those who are alone in the world together with the hope of holy matrimony. Nancy was a retired pastor herself who had a strong heart for the alone and lonely.

A woman who worked alongside Nancy in this ministry was single herself. Her name was Cathy Chun. At some point, with the gentle urging by Nancy, I came to one of her gatherings. I felt that the people who were in attendance were coached to be extra nice to me. As people moved around the room conversing with one another, Cathy came up along with others to talk with me for a while. Cathy was attractive in appearance and in speech.

After the evening, I thought about our encounter for a while. I was also attracted to the strong faith in God that she professed. But it was soon after our loss, and I needed some time before I could start dating. In fact I heard the Lord tell me to wait. I remember in my prayers I asked God if I had to wait, and He said, "Yes." I asked how long? "Three years," He responded. I thought that's too long. But that's what the Lord said, and I needed to be obedient.

Of course, in hindsight, it was necessary. I needed time and space between Asa and myself. The girls, too, needed space between Asa and themselves. I realized that space needed to be created so there was room for another. My daughter Katie was not warm to the idea of remarriage. I remember her saying, "You have us, you don't need another." I said, "It's not the same."

It wasn't until the spring of 2012, after three years, when I asked God if it was time to start dating. He said, "Yes." Nancy Young was preparing for a mainland trip and was planning a last singles gathering before she left. She made sure that Cathy would be there.

I remembered from our first meeting that Cathy had shared that she spent most of her time taking care of her father who was suffering from Alzheimer's disease. I was impressed that he had survived so long - for over 15 years. I could not imagine how difficult that was for her, being her father's primary caregiver.

When we got reacquainted, I asked her how her father was, and she sadly replied that he had died in the past year. I told her I was sorry and simply asked how she was doing. That simple question resulted in an outpouring: all about those who were there together; of his last days; her family history, and their restaurant enterprises.

I was greatly impressed that she too frequented a place I really enjoyed when I was a child at the Ala Moana Shopping Center where the family restaurants were located. There was a ride arcade called Keiki (Children) Land. I thought there was no one left on earth who knew of that place. I loved Keiki Land, because it had kiddie rides that I'll never forget. However, I began to develop a slight grudge of envy against her as she shared how she got to go to the arcade as much as she wanted since her family was always at the mall.

When I was a kid, no matter how hard I tried to make my father take me to this place, I remember going there less than five times in my life. Cathy went there almost every day, with lots of money in her hands for every ride. She roamed freely throughout the mall as her parents were busy running their restaurants.

Now, I found someone with a small but deep connection. I was intrigued and needed to meet with her again. I decided to ask Nancy for her email address. I finally got it about a week later, discovering that Cathy was reluctant to give it to me; not ready herself to start dating again. Finally, after some persuasion, Nancy was permitted to give it to me. It was a good thing too because Nancy was about to leave for her trip to the mainland.

So now that I had her email, how was I going to do this? How was I going to meet her? I felt a little like the Tom Hanks character in *Sleepless in Seattle* when he has to figure out how to date again after several years. In my case it had been many years since the last time I went on a date. I decided to ask her out to coffee at a mutually agreed-upon coffee cafe'. My goal was the purpose of getting to know more about how she took care of her dad, something I was really intrigued about. It was my understanding that most Alzheimer's patients usually do not live beyond ten years with this debilitating disease, so I wanted to know how she and her family cared for her father.

After a few emails back and forth, we decided on a coffee shop closer to her home, one that I thought I knew the location of. Unfortunately, I really I did not know where it was on that day. The shopping center that I thought the cafe' was located in actually had no coffee shop in it at all.

I started to panic as I was frantically driving around. Was I going to be late, or not even show up to this first date? I should note that I didn't even have her cell phone number. If getting her email was difficult, asking for her cell number was unthinkable. I was beginning to think that this was going to end before it even got started.

As sweat poured down my brow, I drove around frantically trying to figure out where this place was. Finally, I drove to a local bank hoping a teller could give me some directions. The teller I spoke to had no clue about where the shopping center was, but thankfully, the customer behind me who overheard our conversation did know, and pointed me in the direction of where the cafe' was.

Soon I was off to the right location. Thankfully, I was not late, but she actually was. After about fifteen minutes I decided to check outside for her in the parking lot. As soon as I walked out of the door Cathy came walking in. She said she was sorry for being late. I was just so happy that we were meeting together. I was so nervous being with her this very first time I decided I would just use $20 bills to buy anything, thinking all I needed to do was collect the change after my purchase.

I was so nervous. We ordered our drinks and proceeded to talk. Like most first dates, it was a little awkward, but time passed on and I started to calm down. Being a little nervous is a good thing right? Then she asked me if I was hungry. I didn't get the message, so I simply said, "No". This was, after all, a coffee date, not a meal which would allow either of us to bail out if the date bombed out.

Before driving to our date I had to rush home from school. It was the last day for teachers and my car was stuffed with boxes of my school stuff, folders and books I accumulated over many years. It was the end of that school year and I was transferring out from that school to another. I got home, took a quick shower and wolfed down a quick peanut butter and jelly sandwich.

Cathy, on the other hand as I later found out, was as hungry as a bear by the time we finished our drinks. She probably wasn't serious about our date just being about coffee. We left the coffee shop and headed to a nearby Taco Bell for a bite, where we continued to talk for another two hours.

I also prayed with her. Yes, we prayed. I wanted to pray with her and let her know that the Lord was close to my heart. We had our bite, but I was so nervous I didn't touch a nacho from my lunch, which was okay because she devoured my food after she ate hers. I was glad she was so comfortable that she felt she could eat my food, too.

After a while, Katie called me asking where I was. The girls had already come home from school on the bus. I told Cathy I should be going home, so as we left the restaurant I walked her to her car. I gave her what I thought was an acceptable goodbye hug, no kiss, just a hug. I felt she was okay with that. Later she told me she was not quite prepared for a goodbye hug. But yay! It was an overall good start.

I did talk to her about caring for her dad. On that day, it was somewhat hard for her to talk about her father's care as she was still grieving over his death. It would take a few more dates and many conversations before she would reveal more about the challenges of his care. But more importantly for Cathy, it opened the door for her own healing over the deep loss of her father. For me, it was the beginning of my relationship with an incredible woman.

CHAPTER TWENTY FIVE

A Real Date - Lunch

Well, coffee and tacos was a success. Now for a real date, but not dinner...dinner was too serious. Lunch, yes, the perfect second date. Armed with her email address, but not her cell phone number, I was emboldened to invite her to lunch, anywhere she wanted. She suggested a dim sum restaurant at Ala Moana Center. I said fine. Lunch is still informal and easier. If it goes down bad you can still bail out in about an hour.

Not having a clue about what to order, she did most of it, but I saw something interesting and new - snow buns. Gladly, she liked it a lot and she was surprised, too, that a non-Chinese person could make a good dim sum selection.

Lunch went well, so I asked her to take a walk around the mall and maybe have dessert at the food court, which she accepted. As we finished our dessert of local ice cream, I was feeling pretty confident about how things were going. I said that I'd like to see her again, to which she replied, "Why?"

"Why?", I asked. She looked at me and said, "Why do you want to see me again?"

I was stunned by such a reply. Not knowing what to say except the truth, I told her, "Because I like you?" She asked further, "So where is this going?" I said, "I don't know". After all this was just lunch. Then she said, "Are you just dating or are you dating for something serious?"

By now, I wasn't feeling too good or confident about this date. After a pause I replied, "Well, I am interested in getting married again." To which she carefully nodded her head, showing that she understood. She then said, "I don't have anything to bring to this relationship." Cathy said this because she was still emotionally drained in the aftermath of losing her father. I don't know how I came up with the words but I said, "That is enough for me."

Wow! This conversation was sure clearing the air. Since we were on topic of some kind of possible relationship, which was looking pretty dismal at that point, I asked her if she had ever married. She said, "No." I then asked her if she had any children, she said, "No."

These were the two best replies I could have ever hoped to get. Not that it's not possible to have a relationship with other circumstances, but her not being previously married, nor having had any children made things a lot less complicated. Yay! Oh good! A bloody honest lunch date - but a real date.

A few more day dates, a walk around magic Island and a trip to the North Shore gave us a lot of time to talk. Then came a big moment. Before a hike to the Makapuu Lighthouse, she invited me to meet her mom.

Okay, this was going to be scary. I remember in high school my friends told me how Chinese parents can be really mean if the boy suitor was not Chinese. This could get ugly. But if I wanted to pursue this relationship, this challenge of meeting her mom needed to be overcome.

I will never forget meeting Mrs. Thelma Chun for the first time. She wore a dark red sweater with immaculate hair. She came out from her bedroom and warmly shook my hand with both of her hands. Then she proceeded to share family pictures and memorabilia contained in the large glass shelf case in the living room.

I listened intently as she proudly shared loving memories of her life and family. Our meeting went totally well and I was so happy that she was so kind to me. This was the beginning of a great, but very short, relationship I had with Cathy's mother. To this day I miss her so much and always will. It was so nice to have a mother again after I lost mine some years ago.

Many dates later Cathy and I found ourselves at our favorite Shopping Center, Ala Moana. We were enjoying a drink at the food court, when I felt I just had to tell her, "I think I am falling in love with you." Hoping she would reply in kind, she just looked away shyly. Boldly, I asked, "Do you love me?" To which she looked down and nodded - yes. I knew it! Yes, she was in love with me too! That was a good day.

BRYAN I. YAMASHITA

CHAPTER TWENTY SIX

Meeting The Girls

We had been on several dates, so it was time for Cathy to meet the girls. We decided that we would go to the Kroc Center together, since I had a family membership and the girls enjoyed the water play area. This had to be a little uncomfortable for Cathy since she didn't swim well, so we planned that we would play only on the shallow side.

Shortly after getting into the water, Katie surprised Cathy with a splash of water to her face. Okay, I thought, this is going to take some time. For whatever reason, this is going to be harder for Katie since she thought we were fine, just the three of us. Remember, she was not warm to the idea of me dating, as she thought that she and Tori were enough for me. Besides, after our loss, Katie moved up to second in command in our family, and she liked it.

Thankfully, Tori was very open to the idea of having a new mom, and therefore was more receptive to Cathy from the beginning. It turned out that those two were very much alike, more emotional. This in comparison to Katie and me, as we are more rational and practical. So it's been a challenge. Even as we are in our fifth year of marriage, Cathy and Tori have grown to have a strong relationship. But it was going to take some time and shared life experiences for Cathy and Katie to get closer.

CHAPTER TWENTY SEVEN

The Proposal

After good rounds of premarital counseling provided by Cathy's close friends from church, we were given a thumbs up to get married. I cannot emphasize enough the need to do premarital counseling. There are many important parts of a marriage that need to be discussed before taking wedding vows. If you can get past the counseling, it will not take all of the potholes out of your marriage, but it will surely make for a smoother ride.

Yay! Now I could finally propose. The engagement ring has always been a mystery to me. How do you size your fiancée's ring finger without giving up the surprise? Anyway, I decided to buy a cheap cosmetic ring for the proposal and later replace it with the real engagement ring. The final questions remaining to be answered: *how* and *where* will I do this?

Of course, this sounds dumb, but it would happen at our favorite childhood place - Keiki Land. The only thing though, was that Keiki Land was gone, and had actually been gone for about 30 years. No matter, the proposal would definitely take place at Ala Moana Center for sure, because this was one of our happy places.

So, I wondered, where would be the most romantic place to pop the big question? Well, I found it. On the third floor on the east side of the mall there is an area between Macy's and the Makai southside stores, a space that overlooks the Ala Wai Boat Harbor and Magic Island. It's beautiful in the day with the park and harbor in the foreground and the ocean in the back. At night, the park and harbor light up with the water glistening by the stars or moonlight. A big Koa bench fronts this area and that would be the spot.

It was a cool November evening. We had just finished dinner and a walk around the mall when I suggested we go to that place. Perfectly, no one was there. We took a seat on the bench and together we gazed out into the harbor and park. Then I took a deep breath, got off the bench and got down on bended knee. I quietly but clearly addressed by her full name - Cathy Laijhun Chun - and requested her hand in marriage to be my wedded wife and the mother of my two girls. She was quiet during my speech, with her head down. When I was done proposing she kept her eyes down and simply nodded - yes.

Yay! She nodded "*Yes*." I took out the ring and she let me slip it on, but of course it was way too big as I had planned. I explained to her that it was just for the proposal and she, the consummate shopper, simply said, "Where did you get this?" Having told her it was from a shop at the mall, within minutes, we were back at the store to look at other cosmetic rings. She would swap this ring for a better fitting one until we got the real one. But no matter, we were now engaged.

CHAPTER TWENTY EIGHT

The Wedding

We got engaged in November, so we thought a six-month engagement would give us enough time to plan our wedding. Honestly, since this was my second wedding, I wanted to do whatever Cathy wanted. This would be her first wedding, hopefully her last, and it had to be special.

I had thought of renting a big house somewhere that could accommodate all of our guests; however, when the idea came up about having the ceremony and reception at her parents' home, it just made a lot of sense. The Chun family home had started as a vacant lot high up on Alewa Heights. Mr. and Mrs. Chun made plans for a grand home, complete with a large dance floor for entertaining. Calvin Chun loved to throw big parties and had a state-of-the-art stereo system for that era installed in the walls so he could play his favorite dance tunes.

Outside of the dance floor was a patio that would take the overflow of the party and allow the guests to cool themselves after "cutting the rug" to one of the dance numbers. Living on a mountain has its advantages. All the music could be played loudly, as any sound would just go out into the great expanse and not really bother any of the neighbors. He also built an outdoor cooking room so he could prepare delicious meals for his guests. He was an amazing self-taught chef. He left his mark on all of his various dishes that came out of his restaurants.

But there were some issues that had to be overcome for the wedding. The wonderful home had come under some disrepair in later years, and needed a lot of love. But it was fun to make repairs, because it was something we could all work on together as a new family.

Big help came from Cathy's sister Patti and husband James. We did a lot of scraping and repainting, retiling, and cleaning. In the end it really looked like the home was brought back to its former glory - something that I feel would have really pleased Cathy's dad if he were alive. Mrs. Chun was so happy, too, to see the home in such a bright condition.

Since we were having our wedding in the family home I decided to keep my guest list very short to allow Cathy the most room for her family and friends. My list was down to just my three brothers and their wives, which included the wedding minister, my brother Boyden. All of my brothers are special to me but Boyden really helped me through our tragedy. He called me every morning for three years just to make sure we were okay.

What a guy! In retrospect, I wish I had invited a few close friends, but, oh well...what was done was done.

Parking was a big concern since there is virtually no street parking in Alewa Heights. The planners of the development only allowed enough space for a road to wind up and down the mountain. After some brainstorming, we decided to ask the Coptic Church at the former Grace Bible Church of Honolulu location to rent parking spaces. We also hired a valet parking company to shuttle our guests up to the house and back to the church parking lot. This worked great as the pastor of the church was more than willing to let us use their parking lot and the Elite valet parking company would accommodate our every need. Praise God, the parking problem was solved.

My dear fiancée, Cathy, being so considerate of the church neighbors, made me create a flyer to warn them of extra traffic that would come on that evening. As we canvassed the nearby homes a month before our wedding, I felt like a political campaigner as we walked from house to house. Most people avoided us but a few we talked to really appreciated our warning.

As we got closer to our wedding it became apparent that this was becoming a Chun family affair. Sister Patti sewed and altered Cathy's wedding dress and those of the bridal party. Sister Charlene and her boyfriend, Chris, were flying in from Maryland to make our wedding cake and dessert cookies. Sister Lynn, a former showcase designer for Macy's, and her husband, Jerry, flew in from San Francisco to decorate the house and help put up the wedding tent. Lynn also designed and printed our invitations.

Cathy's nephew, Travis, and his girlfriend, Amber, provided a magnificent tent for the ceremony along with the benches for our guests to sit on. Amber's mom provided all the long stem roses and flowers that were everywhere on the property. Amber's father handled much of the food service as well as the baking of his yummy bread pudding, which was a great hit. My daughter Katie and her friend Susie Chung cooked made-to-order shrimp pasta which also was a great hit. Among the dishes we served were hot pastrami sliders. These reminded guests of one of the family's restaurants.

Everything went well except the weather. The skies started to pour right up to the ceremony. That was when God's hand came down to hold back the rain. It probably helped that we had a few pastors and their wives in attendance who probably prayed fervently to stop the rain, at least for the ceremony, which it did.

What I remember most from the ceremony was the smile on my mother-in-law's face as she walked Cathy down the aisle. At 95 years of age she beamed with pride that she could see her last daughter get married. What I also remember most was kissing Cathy for the first time at the end of the ceremony. We decided on a no kissing policy before the wedding to help us keep from any temptation of doing anything more. I highly recommend this as well.

There was so much more about how God blessed our wedding. It was just amazing how things fall into place. We learned the more you get to know God, and trust in him, the more you know how amazing He really is.

CHAPTER TWENTY NINE

Losing Thelma Chun

One of the hardest things during the first year of our marriage was the passing of my mother-in-law, Thelma Chun. From the first time I met her, I knew she was a very special person, one I grew to love, and cherish. She had long since retired from her apparel business and her work at the family restaurant. She was enjoying her final years in the comfort of her home, in the care of her daughters. Since it was necessary to spend the nights with her, and now that Cathy and I were married and living in Ewa Beach, sister Patti and Cathy worked out a schedule of sleeping over to keep Mom company.

When it was our turn, it was fun for the girls as we would all pack up and stay for the weekend at grandma's house. On one weekend while Hawaii was threatened by two hurricanes, we emptied our own freezer and cooked and ate everything at grandma's house. In the evenings we got together on the carpet to camp out and watch the Lord of the Rings trilogy, extended version. Now that was a lot of fun.

Unfortunately, in November of that year, 2014, the morning after a family dinner at a favorite restaurant, Mom had a severe stroke that made her unconscious. By that evening she had passed away in the presence of Patti, after Cathy and I left the room for a while.

Thelma Chun was an amazing woman and had an incredible life. She had lost her own mother at the age of five and she was raised in a boarding school by nuns. She got married and had four beautiful daughters. She ran her own Hawaiian apparel business, and took care of her husband's businesses in the evenings. Whenever a man can claim success in life, you know there is a special woman who supported that success all along the way. Thelma Chun was that special woman.

I will always miss my mother-in-law, but not nearly as much as her daughters do. But I will always be grateful for being accepted by her and loved by her too.

CHAPTER THIRTY

Life Changes That Cause Stress

It wasn't until after Mom left us, that I realized how much Cathy went through in a few years. After living at home her whole life, she took care of her parents, including her father who had Alzheimer's disease. She lost him in 2011, dated me in 2012, married me in 2014 and changed her name; became a wife and stepmother to my daughters and ended the year with her mom's passing; I'd say that's a lot to have lived through.

On a chart used to measure stress, these life changes would take a person right off of it. She saw a therapist to help her through these life changes, but I know God helped her the most. It was her faith in the Lord Jesus Christ that got her through so much.

She knew she was destined to marry one day, an event that was prophesied over twelve years prior at a Christian prophetic conference. The prophet told her that she would marry and that the suitor would seek or pursue her and that she would not have to do anything. A week later, after the conference, she asked God when this guy would come. Well, after some years and the need to provide extreme care for her father she was resigned to simply stay single, if that was what the Lord wanted for her.

But God cannot lie, His promises are always true. It just took a while - well, years, actually - but the prophecy came true. After meeting her previously twice before, I was ready, as the Lord said I would be, to date again, and pursue her.

Here we are in our sixth year of marriage, and, as I am writing this book, I am blessed to say Cathy is a great wife and mother to Katie and Tori. She has moved to Ewa Beach from a life of being a "townie" from Honolulu. She has credited stores like *Ross' Dress For Less* for softening her adjustment to the west side. I am so glad she likes living on this side of the island, and yes we have a lot more retail stores than we did before.

She still dearly misses her parents, Calvin and Thelma Chun, but we know we will see them again when Jesus returns, since both were saved. A wonderful thing that I truly support is an annual trip that Cathy and her sisters take each year around May to get together for a week or so. My brothers-in-law tag along, but it's a great time for the sisters to bond together as they mature, and allow them to reminisce about their parents.

The next big event of Cathy's life and that of the girls was when she legally adopted them. After we got married and transitioned into our new life together I started to realize the limitations of step-parenting. In our school complex, step parents are not allowed to sign field trip forms or sign excuse notes. Also, step parents cannot make medical appointments for the children. Clearly, the authority of a step parent in Hawaii can be very limited.

It was about three years into our marriage when I asked Cathy about legally adopting the girls. I began the conversation by asking whether she loved the girls, to which she did not answer. She then explained that she loved me and married me but did not really see the girls as her own. She asked me, "Do they love me?" I said, "Maybe they don't." When we got married I made it clear to the girls that Cathy was now their mom, and that in our home I would give her full authority over them as if what she said came from me. However, this policy only works in our home. Plus, love cannot be forced. God gave us free will, so we also are free to choose who we love.

But who chose to love first? Did God love us first or did we love him first? Of course, God loved us first. God the Father in Heaven loved us first, before we were even born. He made us in our mothers' wombs. I explained to Cathy, as God loved us first, we as parents must love our children first before our children can love us. When babies are born, are they wired to start loving their parents? No, there is nothing they can do in the way of love. As they witness the work of our creator, parents naturally fall in love with their children first.

In a few months, after much prayer and spending time with God, Cathy confessed that, yes, she loved the girls as her own, as her God loved her. She was ready to legally adopt them. Well, like a lot of things Cathy does, she gets right on it. Sometimes she thinks she can be a bit too obsessive. I like to say she gets focused.

Anyway, after a few calls to prominent attorneys regarding adoption, it became apparent that this case would be complicated because the girls were foreign-born, from China, and that their previous adoptive mother had died. It seemed nobody wanted to touch our case.

We decided to go online and start the process anyway by filling out the legal forms on our own. Funny, all the forms had to be hand-printed, since hardly anyone has typewriters anymore. Boy, did I need to brush up on my handwriting skills! I discovered that they were as bad as they had been in grade school. My handwriting pieces were always the ones singled out by my teachers to be the samples that should never be modeled.

Finally, we got the forms we thought we needed done, and Cathy made a trip to family court to process the papers. There, to our great relief, was a court clerk who was so helpful that she said we could call her on her cell phone anytime if we should have any questions about the process. She looked at our papers and kindly told us what corrections we needed to get done and gave us additional forms to be filled out. She admitted that she had never dealt with a case like ours but said that somehow it will all work out, which it did.

After about a month after our last submittal, the court clerk called us with the great news that the paperwork was approved, and that we would get a court date in about six months. In March of 2017, we were given our day in Family Court. The presiding judge looked through our papers and then looked up at me. I think he recognized me from our previous tragedy. After a while, he said, "Everything's going to be approved, we just need to have some questions answered."

He looked at me and said, "Just realize that after today, if anything should happen (i.e. divorce), your wife will get custody of the girls." I could not help but smile at his announcement. Each of the girls gave their consent to the legal adoption by Cathy; to no longer be their stepmother, but simply be their *mother* as the court only recognizes one mother and one father. After our time in court, we paused to take a few selfies in front of the courthouse and celebrated our first day as a legal family with a great dinner. Yay!

CHAPTER THIRTY ONE

Happily Ever After - Not

I wish I could say we live a perfect life, happily ever after. Honestly, it's as close as I could ever imagine, through the grace of our Lord Jesus Christ, who Himself is perfect.

When I began this journey of seeking a new wife and mother for my girls, I had this vision of a car changing its wheel and tire while it was still moving.

I have actually seen this done on TV a long time ago when I was a kid. This creative fellow devised a way of changing his wheel while his car was still moving by lifting the car with a special jack set above two other wheels, then setting up a ramp outside of the wheel for him to stand on allowing him to change the wheel and then installing the spare, and then lowering it down on the road without stopping at all.

Getting married again was kind of like that. Sometimes life does not pause for us to make changes. Sometimes we must make changes as life changes. Of course, it can be rather complicated, but with God all things are possible.

Like all marriages, ours continues to mature. We just celebrated our 5th anniversary at this writing. We have our bumps and scrapes, but we try to reconcile our conflicts, or at least be in the process of reconciliation, before we say *goodnight*.

I, for myself, have taken one word from my marriage vows to heart, and that word is *cherish*. At the end of the day I always ask myself, "Did I cherish Cathy today?" Did I show in actions and words that she is special to me, worthy of my special care? It is a high bar to set, one that I rarely accomplish, but one that I feel puts her life as my wife where it should be, at a very high place.

Although I thought I was a pretty good husband before, I definitely want to be a better one today and tomorrow. I believe it pleases my Lord that I take care of my wife this way. Being her husband is not only a holy responsibility, but an honor bestowed on me by God. Therefore, I think that a true measure of a man, or husband, depends on the well-being of his wife.

Raising two teenage girls while being newlyweds had its challenges. Between the physical, social, and emotional changes Katie and Tori are going through, bringing a new wife and mother into the mix can be very challenging to say the least. But anything good takes time, tons of love and grace, while at times, suffering. But it is nothing compared to the suffering of our Lord Jesus Christ and His work on the cross. His suffering gives us strength and hope through any trials and challenges that come our way.

All I can say is that I am truly grateful to my Lord God for all that He has done for myself and my family. He is faithful even when I am not. Whatever faith I have in Him, pleases Him, and His response has always been overwhelming. Our family mantra continues to be to *believe, trust, and obey God.*

As I continue my walk in life with the Lord I look forward to His continued presence in it, sometimes leading me, sometimes correcting me, and sometimes providing and protecting me by His love and grace.

CHAPTER THIRTY TWO

Spiritual Support

I would like to write more about the support I received while in my walk with Jesus Christ. Funny, one of the greatest sources of spiritual support came from the radio. Asa never mentioned it but she had one of her radio buttons set on K-Love, which is a nationally syndicated Christian music radio station. I discovered the station while driving her car after her death. I have never stopped listening to the station ever since.

I discovered so much music that sustained me in the aftermath of our experience; music that spoke the truth about what happened. Notable artists like Jeremy Camp, who lost his first wife, spoke to my situation and his music would always bring me to tears. Music also by Steven Curtis Chapman, especially his CD in the aftermath of his own family tragedy, sung to the depths of my own heart. A dear friend of mine tried to listen to the CD but could not get past the second song. This music is a dark journey into Steven's experience. There was a time I played this CD over and over many times and it always brought me to tears and touched the depths of my soul.

In the aftermath of our tragedy my nightly bedtime Bible reading went on a whole new level. Every word that I read had new meanings and understandings that I never had before. I believe trusting in God allowed me greater insight into God's love, purpose, and Kingdom.

A special thanks goes to churches we've attended as a family. This includes Nu'uanu Congregational Church, Pearl City

Community Church and Grace Bible Kapolei. We currently attend and serve at Grace Bible Church Pearlside, headed by senior pastor Norman Nakanishi. But the fellow Christian I am most close to actually has his home in my neighborhood. His name is Pastor Eric Ebisu. He is a missionary in Japan, along with some of his family. Pastor Eric is a true man of God who is always gentle and soft spoken but is a fiery believer of the Gospel and a defender of the *word*. I call him a faithful friend and a close brother in Christ.

CHAPTER THIRTY THREE

A Special Mahalo: Thanks

I cannot end this book without expressing my most humble appreciation to those who expressed their concern for us through our tragedy. On the day Asa died, I felt we were very alone in our tragedy. Having come home that afternoon after picking up the girls, I had spoken to very few people. It wasn't until the next day that I began to learn how this event was becoming big news.

By the end of Asa's memorial service we began to understand how so many people, many complete strangers, cared for us. Our spare room was filled with a multitude of gifts: books, toys, candies and snacks of every kind. Again, I want to take this opportunity to express my sincere appreciation to the people of Hawaii who expressed their condolences in so many ways - prayers, cards, gifts, and best wishes for myself and my family.

Most of all, I thank God Almighty, his son Jesus Christ and the Holy Spirit for his steadfast faithfulness and amazing grace and love for us all.

CHAPTER THIRTY FOUR

The Last Word

Finally, I just want to end that on that fateful day of our tragedy, I felt like my back was pushed to the very edge of a high precipice. I was given a choice: in front of me was a thread of faith to cling to, and in back of me was darkness and the abyss. I chose to grab that thread of faith in God because it was really all I could do.

I pray that I will always choose the Lord today, tomorrow, and forevermore. This choice is yours as well. Please choose wisely. Choose wisely because we all are given a choice to either believe in an all-powerful God, or not to believe. This all powerful God is known as the creator and maker of the earth and the universe. He gives us His name, one of which is "Yahweh." He gives us his name so we can call him by name, and not be confused by other gods. To those who believe in Him, He is known as the Father in heaven. The Father who gave his only son - Jesus - to die for our sins.

He died for sins we all have committed since the beginning, with the first man - Adam. Sins are all the things we do, or think of doing, that mean harm to others, or ourselves, and displease the Father. Asa's death was a result of the sins of our broken world.

The Father sent His son Jesus to die over 2000 years ago. If anyone believes in Him, they will be forgiven, saved from hell and will go on to live in heaven forever. To ultimately be in heaven with Jesus requires nothing be done, since His sacrifice was a gift. All you can, or need to do is simply accept this incredible gift and believe and trust in Him. I leave you with the last word, and the last word is to believe in Christ *Jesus*.

APPENDIX

My Daily Prayer

Dear God, my Father in heaven, please hear my prayer.

Praise You and Your holy name.

Praise You in the highest heavens, praise Your hand and arm on earth.

Praise the one who comes in the name of the LORD, the Lord of heaven's armies,

the God of Abraham, Isaac, and Jacob, and Israel.

Please bless this day by Your will and way, and may our will and our way be one with Yours through the Holy Spirit.

Please bless this new day as it unfolds.

Please bless my family, neighbors, friends, those in need, those who are ill.

Please bless my local church, The Pearlside Church; the staff, servants, and congregation.

Please bless our state, country, and world.

Thank You for last night and yesterday.

Please accept the prayer that Jesus taught us as he said:

Our Father who art in heaven, hallowed be thy name.

Thy kingdom come, thy will be done, on earth as it is in heaven.

Give us this day our daily bread and forgive us our debts as we forgive our debtors.

And lead us not into temptation, but deliver us from evil.

For thine is the kingdom, the power, and the glory forever. Amen.

Thank You Jesus for this prayer, thank You God, and thank You Holy Spirit.

God bless the Father and His holy name, the Son, and the Holy Spirit.

In the name of Jesus we pray, Amen.

The following is a poem written by Alyssa De Mello, daughter of Tim and Cora De Mello which was printed and shared at Asa's Memorial Service. The poem speaks of what happened from six perspectives. The first is mine, the second is Katie's, the third is Tori's, the fourth is Asa's, the fifth is God's, and the sixth is hers.

Beauty From Pain

It's surreal. Just a big dream I can't wait to wake up from... it can't be true, it just can't. How can it be that you are no longer here? You just slipped through my very grasp. A few moments away from having you in my arms once more. This wasn't what we had planned but I know no matter what I do, you can't come back... Here I am, still clinging onto the day I will see you once again. And after my eyes have cried their last tear, your heart's beauty will bring me through all of the pain...

You touched many lives and it's incredible how you still are. Lives of strangers have been changed through this tragedy and from your love. You touched my life as well... I never got to tell you how much you changed my life; even if it was just from reading a simple book. Your voice will forever be engraved in my mind and your presence with me always. I know you don't want to be grieved over, but just, loved and remembered always. So...I LOVE You!

We were chosen special by you. You brought us into your life and took on a big responsibility. It just isn't right for this to have happened. We will cherish every memory we had together. Even though you weren't here for long, your

Love surrounds us always. We miss you so... it shouldn't have happened in the first place, but we must accept that it did indeed occur. It is incredibly hard to be without you but we know you are always with us. Even if it's just in our hearts, our memories, or even our family pictures...

I was taken by surprise. I wasn't completely aware of what had happened. But I do now. It is difficult to explain. I love you so much and will forever be your guardian angel. I am amazed with the impact that this simple life has made. It's a God thing for sure...

She is my child and I love her dearly. She is in better hands now and feels no pain. She has made a great addition to the beauty of Heaven. She's seen how your lives have been impacted and so have I. You are all blessed to have known her and now I get to spend my time with her. Do not woe for she is in a place that is beautiful. Do not worry for she knows how much you love her. She hears your prayers and messages. Her heart is touched by you just as much as she has yours. Don't forget that you're only a second away from her love...

I admit this is a rough time. We won't forget her. This I know is certain. And when someone asks You how you got through it, how you survived, just say, "If dust can be made into something beautiful, why can't a tragedy?" HIS love got you through this. Not just hers... Remember the beauty of it... not just the pain.

Alyssa De Mello, 13 years

ABOUT THE AUTHOR

BRYAN I. YAMASHITA

Bryan is a retired teacher who resides in Ewa Beach (Oahu), Hawaii with his wife and two daughters. He enjoys serving in the shuttle ministry at Pearlside Church, a yard work ministry, body surfing, fishing and sweeping out his garage as he listens to George Strait.

www.ingramcontent.com/pod-product-compliance
Lightning Source LLC
Chambersburg PA
CBHW050322120526
44592CB00014B/2016